JAMESTOWN EDUCATION

Reading in the Content Areas
SCIENCE

Based on the work of Walter Pauk

Mc Graw Hill **Glencoe**

New York, New York   Columbus, Ohio   Chicago, Illinois   Peoria, Illinois   Woodland Hills, California

JAMESTOWN EDUCATION

Readability

Tab 1: Levels D–F
Tab 2: Levels G–I
Tab 3: Levels J–K
Tab 4: Levels L–L+

Cover photo: © Don Grall/Index Stock Imagery

Mc Graw Hill Glencoe

The McGraw·Hill Companies

ISBN: 0-07-861707-3

Send all queries to:
Glencoe/McGraw-Hill
8787 Orion Place
Columbus, OH 43240-4027

5 6 7 8 9 10 079 08 07 06

Contents

To the Student

To succeed in the courses you take, one of the most important skills you can have is good reading ability. Different courses require different types of reading. If material is easy for you or you have studied it before, you may read quickly. If the material is new or difficult, you may read slowly. In fact, you may read the material several times. You can use the reading skills featured in this book in all your courses.

The passages in the book are readings in science. Within this subject area are several subcategories, including biology, weather, and scientific laws.

This book does not require you to master many new facts. Instead, its purpose is to show you *how to read science-related information.* You will learn techniques that textbook writers use to organize material. You will see how new information can be added to what you already know. And you will learn about the six skills that can help you read just about anything.

The Six Types of Questions

In this book, the basic skills necessary for reading factual material are taught through the use of the following six types of questions: main idea, subject matter, supporting details, conclusion, clarifying devices, and vocabulary in context.

Main Idea. Whenever you read, ask yourself, What point is the writer trying to make? If you look for an answer to this question, you will probably find one. But if you don't focus, all things may seem equal. Nothing will stand out.

Try to find the main idea in the following passage by asking yourself, What point is the writer trying to make?

> The worker ants in an ant colony have many different jobs. Some workers pull the eggs from the royal chamber into a room called the nursery. There they help larvae climb out of their shells. In the nursery, there are workers who look after the larvae until they become full-grown ants. Some workers look for food and store it in the granary, where seeds are kept. Others dump leftovers in the rubbish room. Ants have their own complete, busy world hidden in tunnels under our feet!

What is the main idea? Here's a good answer: Worker ants do many different jobs in an ant colony. This passage is fairly easy to figure out because the first sentence is an excellent topic sentence.

The next example does not have a topic sentence. Nevertheless you can still answer the question, What point is the writer trying to make? This time, think about the passage and come up with your own answer.

The furry platypus, a native of Australia and Tasmania, looks like a mammal at first glance. Upon studying it more closely, however, one recognizes the birdlike characteristics that have puzzled scientists. For example, like some water birds, the playpus has webbed feet. It also has a leathery bill like a duck. That's how the animal got its name, the "duck-billed platypus." In addition, the semi-aquatic platypus lays eggs like a bird.

This passage may have required a bit more thought, as the correct answer is a summary type answer. Compare your answer with the following main idea statement: The furry platypus looks like a mammal but has several birdlike characteristics.

Subject Matter. This question looks easy and often is easy. But don't let that fool you into thinking it isn't important. The subject matter question can help you with the most important skill of all in reading and learning: concentration. With it, you comprehend and learn. Without it, you fail.

Here is the secret for concentrating: After reading a few lines of a passage, ask yourself, What is the subject matter of this passage? Instantly you will be thinking about the passage. You will be concentrating. If you don't ask this question, your eyes may move across the print, yet your mind may be thinking of other things.

By asking this question as you read each passage in this book, you will master the skill so well that it will carry over to everything you read.

Let's see how this method works. Here is a short passage.

The moon circles Earth on the average of once every 29 days. Its orbit around Earth is not circular; it is oval. The moon's distance from Earth can vary quite a bit. Sometimes the moon is 250,000 miles from Earth. Other times it is only 220,000 miles away.

On finishing the first sentence, you may have thought, *Ah, a passage on the moon going around Earth. Maybe I can learn something about this process.* If it was, your head was in the right place. By focusing right away on the subject matter, you will be concentrating, you will be looking for something, and—best of all—you will be understanding, learning, and remembering.

Supporting Details. In common usage, the word *detail* has taken on the meaning of "something relatively unimportant." But details are important. Details are the plaster, board, and brick of a building, while main ideas are the large strong steel or wooden beams. A solid, well-written passage must contain both.

The bulk of a factual passage is made up of details that support the main idea. The main idea is often buried among the details. You have to dig to distinguish between the main idea and the details. Here are some characteristics that can help you see the difference between supporting details and main ideas.

First, supporting details come in various forms. They can be examples, explanations, descriptions, definitions, comparisons, contrasts, exceptions, analogies, similes, and metaphors.

Second, these various kinds of details are used to support the main idea. The words themselves—*supporting details*—spell out their job. So when you have trouble finding the main idea, take a passage apart sentence by sentence. Ask yourself, Does this sentence support something, or is this the idea being supported? In other words, you must not only separate the main idea from the details, but you must also see how they help one another. The main idea can often be expressed in a single sentence. But a sentence cannot tell a complete story. The writer must use additional sentences to give a full picture.

The following passage shows how important details are for providing a full picture of what the writer had in mind.

> The woodpecker pecks at a speed of 1,300 miles per hour. At this speed, the impact of the bird's beak hitting the wood is almost like the impact of a supersonic jet smashing into a mountain. Each peck takes just a thousandth of a second. The movement is quicker than the human eye can follow. Incredibly, the bird's cherry-sized brain is never injured from all this furious smashing.

The main idea is in the first sentence. After stating the main idea, the writer gives several examples showing why it is true. The examples are supporting details.

Conclusion. As a reader moves through a passage, grasping the main idea and the supporting details, it is natural for him or her to begin to guess an ending or a conclusion. Some passages contain conclusions; others do not. It all depends on the writer's purpose. For example, some passages simply describe a process—how something is done. It is not always necessary to draw a conclusion from such a passage.

In some passages with conclusions, the writer states the conclusion. But in most passages in this book, the conclusion is merely implied. That is, the writer seems to have come to a conclusion but has not stated it. It is up to you to draw that conclusion.

In the following passage, the writer implies a conclusion but does not state it directly.

> The elephant's great size can sometimes present a heat problem. The larger an object, the more difficulty it has losing heat. Elephants live on the hot plains of Africa, where keeping cool is not an easy task. Elephants' huge ears help them cool their bodies so they can survive in the heat. The large surfaces of the ears have many blood vessels that are very close to the surface of the skin. Blood that is closer to the surface cools more easily.

From this passage, we can draw the conclusion that, without their large ears, elephants probably would not survive in the African heat.

Sometimes a writer will ask you to draw a conclusion by applying what you have learned to a new situation, as in the following passage.

> Odd as it sounds, orange growers use ice to fight freezing! Some spray their crops with water on freezing nights. The water freezes quickly, and then a strange thing happens. As long as ice stays wet, it can't get colder than 32 degrees Fahrenheit. Trees and oranges can stand this temperature. But if the ice dries and becomes entirely frozen, the temperature can drop many degrees and the crop would be ruined. The trick is to spray water on the ice continuously. The spraying keeps the temperature from going below 32 degrees even if the air is much colder. This strange kind of "ice blanket" works only on plants strong enough to stand the weight of frozen spray.

Looking for a conclusion puts you in the shoes of a detective. While reading, you have to think, *Where is the writer leading me? What conclusion will I be able to draw?* And, like a detective, you must try to guess the conclusion, changing the guess as you get more and more information.

Clarifying Devices. Clarifying devices are words, phrases, and techniques that a writer uses to make main ideas and supporting details clear and interesting. By knowing some of these clarifying and controlling devices, you will be better able to recognize them in the passages you read. By recognizing them, you will be able to read with greater comprehension and speed.

Transitional or Signal Words. The largest single group of clarifying devices, and the most widely used, is transitional or signal words. Here are some signal words that you see all the time: *first, second, next, last,* and *finally.* A writer uses such words to keep ideas, steps in a process, or lists in order. Other transitional words include *however, in brief, in conclusion, above all, therefore, since, because,* and *consequently.*

When you see transitional words, consider what they mean. A transitional word like *or* tells you that another option, or choice, is coming. Words like *but* and *however* signal that a contrast, or change in point of view, will follow.

Organizational Patterns. Organizational patterns are also clarifying devices. One such pattern is the chronological pattern, in which events unfold in the order of time: one thing happens first, then another, and another, and so on. A time pattern orders events. The incident may take place in five minutes or over a period of hundreds of years.

There are other organizational patterns as well. Writers may use spatial descriptions to tell what things look like. They may use lists of examples to make their point. In science writing, they may use scientific data. Seeing the organizational pattern will help you read the material more easily.

Textual Devices. Textbook writers often use patterns or particular text styles to make their ideas clear. Bulleted lists, subheads, and boldfaced or italicized words help to highlight important ideas in the text. Concepts shown in charts or diagrams may be easier to understand than concepts explained in words alone.

Literal Versus Figurative Language. Sometimes a writer's words do not mean exactly what they seem to on first reading. For example, a writer may say, "The great tragedy shattered the hero of the story." You may know *shattered* as meaning "breaking into pieces." The word is often applied to breakable objects, but here it is applied to a person's feelings. Being alert to such special meanings of words can help you appreciate the writer's meaning.

Two literary devices that writers use to present ideas in interesting ways are similes (SIM-a-leez) and metaphors (MET-a-forz). Both are used to make comparisons that add color and power to ideas. A simile always uses the word *like* or *as*. Here's an example of a simile: She has a mind like a computer. In this simile, a person's mind is compared to a computer. The metaphor, on the other hand, makes a direct comparison: Her mind is a computer.

Vocabulary in Context. How accurate are you in using words you think you already know? Do you know that the word *exotic* means "a thing or a person from a foreign country"? Exotic flowers and exotic costumes are flowers and costumes from foreign countries. *Exotic* has been used incorrectly so often and for so long that it has developed a second meaning. Many people use *exotic* to mean "strikingly unusual, as in color or design."

Many people think that the words *imply* and *infer* mean the same thing. They do not. A writer may imply, or suggest, something. The reader then infers what the writer implied. In other words, to imply is to "suggest an idea." To infer is to "take meaning out" or to "draw a conclusion."

It is easy to see what would happen to a passage if a reader skipped a word or two that he or she did not know and imposed fuzzy meanings on a few others. The result would inevitably be a gross misunderstanding of the writer's message. You will become a better reader if you learn the exact meanings and the various shades of meaning of the words that are already familiar to you.

In this book, you should be able to figure out the meanings of many words from their context—that is, from the words and phrases around them. If this method does not work for you, however, you may consult a dictionary.

Answering the Main Idea Question

The main idea questions in this book are not the usual multiple-choice variety that asks you to select the one correct statement. Rather, you are given three statements and are asked to select the statement that expresses the main idea of the passage, the statement that is too narrow, and the statement that is too broad. You have to work hard to identify all three statements correctly. This new type of question teaches you to recognize the differences between statements that, at first, seem almost equal.

To help you handle these questions, let's go behind the scenes to see how the main idea questions in this book were constructed. The true main idea statement was always written first. It had to be neat and succinct. The main idea tells who or what is the subject of the passage. The main idea statement also tells what the subject is doing or what the subject is like. Next, keeping the main idea statement in mind, the other two statements were written. They are variations of the main idea statement. The "too narrow" statement had to express only part of the main idea. The "too broad" statement had to be very general in scope.

Read the passage below. Then, to learn how to answer the main idea questions, follow the instructions in the box. The answer to each part of the question has been filled in for you. The score for each answer has also been marked.

The Dragonfly's Life Cycle

By far the scariest thing about the dragonfly is its name. This double-winged fast-flying insect is totally harmless. It has large, deep eyes that can detect the smallest movements. Its body may be bright blue and red or vivid green. Dragonflies in flight look like dancing spots of color in the light of a midsummer's day.

The dragonfly has a long and respectable history. It was one of the first flying insects on the earth. To see this oldster of the insect world in action, head for a pond. Dragonflies live near water. In fact, they lay their eggs right in the water.

A dragonfly goes through several big changes before it becomes a flying insect. From the egg, a tiny creature called a nymph is hatched. It lives in the water, eating other small creatures that live in the pond. As the nymph grows, it becomes too big for its skin. Then it sheds the skin that is too small for it. Soon it grows a new skin. This <u>molting</u> happens several times, until the insect is full-grown. Then the full-grown insect crawls up the stem of a water plant, out into the air. It squeezes its way out of its last skin as a full-fledged dragonfly.

After going through all that work to grow up, the dragonfly lives for only about a month. But for this short time it startles the hot summer air with its bright beauty.

	Answer	Score
Mark the *main idea*	M	15
Mark the statement that is *too broad*	B	5
Mark the statement that is *too narrow*	N	5

a. Dragonflies are beautiful harmless insects with an interesting life cycle.   M   15

[This statement gathers all the important points. It gives a correct picture of the main idea in a brief way: (1) Dragonflies, (2) harmless and beautiful, (3) interesting life cycle.]

b. Dragonflies lay their eggs in water.   N   5

[This statement is correct, but it is too narrow. It refers to only a part of the dragonfly's life cycle.]

c. Insects that live near water are harmless and fascinating.   B   5

[This statement is too broad. It speaks only of harmless insects, not of dragonflies in particular.]

Getting the Most Out of This Book

The following steps could be called "tricks of the trade." Your teachers might call them "rules for learning." It doesn't matter what they are called. What does matter is that they work.

Think about the title. A famous language expert proposes the following "trick" to use when reading. "The first thing to do is to read the title. Then spend a few moments thinking about it."

Writers spend much time thinking up good titles. They try to pack a lot of meaning into them. It makes sense, for you to spend a few seconds trying to dig out some meaning. These moments of thought will give you a head start on a passage.

Thinking about the title can help you in another way too. It helps you concentrate on a passage before you begin reading. Why does this happen? Thinking about the title fills your head with thoughts about the passage. There's no room for anything else to get in to break your concentration.

The Dot Step. Here is a method that will speed up your reading. It also builds comprehension at the same time.

Spend a few moments with the title. Then read quickly through the passage. Next, without looking back, answer the six questions by placing a dot in the box next to each answer of your choice. The dots will be your "unofficial" answers. For the main idea question (question 1), place your dot in the box next to the statement that you think is the main idea.

The dot system helps by making you think hard on your first fast reading. The practice you gain by trying to grasp and remember ideas makes you a stronger reader.

The Checkmark Step. First, answer the main idea question. Follow the steps that are given above each set of statements for this question. Use a capital letter to mark your final answer to each part of the main idea question.

You have answered the other five questions with a dot. Now read the passage once more carefully. This time, mark your final answer to each question by placing a checkmark (√) in the box next to the answer of your choice. The answers with the checkmarks are the ones that will count toward your score.

The Diagnostic Chart. Now move your final answers to the Diagnostic Chart for the passage. These charts start on page 155.

Use the row of boxes beside Passage 1 for the answers to the first passage. Use the row of boxes beside Passage 2 for the answers to the second passage, and so on. Write the letter of your answer to the left of the dotted line in each block.

Correct your answers using the Answer Keys on pages 152–154. When scoring your answers, do not use an *x* for incorrect or a *c* for correct. Instead, use this method: If your choice is incorrect, write the letter of the correct answer to the right of the dotted line in the block.

Thus, the row of answers for each passage will show your incorrect answers. And it will also show the correct answers.

Your Total Comprehension Score. Go back to the passage you have just read. If you answered a question incorrectly, draw a line under the correct choice on the question page. Then write your score for each question on the line provided. Add the scores to get your total comprehension score. Enter that number in the box marked Total Score.

Graphing Your Progress. After you have found your total comprehension score, turn to the Progress Graphs that begin on page 158. Write your score in the box under the number of the passage. Then put an *x* along the line above the box to show your total comprehension score. Join the *x*'s as you go. This will plot a line showing your progress.

Taking Corrective Action. Your incorrect answers give you a way to teach yourself how to read better. Take the time to study these answers.

Go back to the questions. For each question you answered wrong, read the correct answer (the one you have underlined) several times. With the correct answer in mind, go back to the passage itself. Read to see why the given answer is better. Try to see where you made your mistake. Try to figure out why you chose an incorrect answer.

The Steps in a Nutshell
Here's a quick review of the steps to follow. Following these steps is the way to get the most out of this book. Be sure you have read and understood everything in this To the Student section before you begin reading the passage.

1. **Think about the title of the passage.** Try to get all the meaning the writer put into it.
2. **Read the passage quickly.**
3. **Answer the questions, using the dot system.** Use dots to mark your unofficial answers. Don't look back at the passage.
4. **Read the passage again—carefully.**
5. **Mark your final answers.** Put a checkmark (√) in the box to note your final answer. Use capital letters for each part of the main idea question.
6. **Mark your answers on the diagnostic chart.** Record your final answers on the diagnostic chart for the passage. Write your answers to the left of the dotted line in the answer blocks for the passage.
7. **Correct your answers.** Use the answer keys on pages 152–154. If an answer is not correct, write the correct answer on the right side of the block, beside your incorrect answer. Then go back to the question page. Place a line under the correct answer.
8. **Find your total comprehension score.** Find this by adding up the points you earned for each question. Enter the total in the box marked Total Score.
9. **Graph your progress.** Enter and plot your score on the progress graph for that passage.
10. **Take corrective action.** Read your wrong answers. Read the passage once more. Try to figure out why you were wrong.

To the Teacher

The Reading Passages

Each of the 75 passages included in the book is related to science. Within this subject area are several subcategories, for example, biology, weather, and scientific laws.

Each passage had to meet the following two criteria: high interest level and appropriate readability level. The high interest level was assured by choosing passages of mature content that would appeal to a wide range of readers.

The readability level of each passage was computed by applying Dr. Edward B. Fry's *Formula for Estimating Readability.* The passages are arranged within the book according to reading levels. *Reading in the Content Areas: Science* contains 75 passages that range from reading level 4 to reading level 12+. The passages are organized into four ranges of reading levels, as indicated by color tabs: The first passages range from reading level 4 to reading level 6. The next passages range from reading level 7 to reading level 9. The third group of passages ranges from reading level 10 to reading level 11. The final passages range from reading level to reading level 12+.

The Six Questions

This book is organized around six essential questions. The most important of these is the main idea question, which is actually a set of three statements. Students must first choose and label the statement that expresses the main idea of the passage; then they must label each of the other statements as either too narrow or too broad to be the main idea.

In addition to the main idea question, there are five other questions. These questions are within the framework of the following five categories: subject matter, supporting details, conclusion, clarifying devices, and vocabulary in context.

By repeated practice with answering the questions within these six categories, students will develop an active searching attitude about what they read. These six types of questions will help them become aware of what they are reading at the time they are actually seeing the words and phrases on a page. This thinking-while-reading sets the stage for higher comprehension and better retention.

The Diagnostic Chart

The Diagnostic Chart provides the most dignified form of guidance yet devised. With this chart, no one has to point out a student's weaknesses. The chart does that automatically, yielding the information directly and personally to the student, making self-teaching possible. The organization of the questions and the format for marking answers on the chart are what make it work so well.

The six questions for each passage are always in the same order. For example, the question designed to teach the skill of drawing conclusions is always the fourth question, and the main idea question is always first. Keeping the questions in order sets the stage for the smooth working of the chart.

The chart works automatically when students write the letter of their answer choices for each passage in the spaces provided. Even after completing only one passage, the chart will reveal the types of questions answered correctly as well as the types answered incorrectly. As the answers for more passages are recorded, the chart will show the types of questions that are missed consistently. A pattern can be seen after three or more passages have been completed. For example, if a student answers question 4 (drawing conclusions) incorrectly for three out of four passages, the student's weakness in this area shows up automatically.

Once a weakness is revealed, have your students take the following steps: First, turn to the instructional pages in the beginning of the book and study the section in which the topic is discussed. Second, go back and reread the questions that were missed in that particular category. Then, with the correct answer to a question in mind, read the entire passage again, trying to see how the writer developed the answer to the question. Do this for each question that was missed. Third, when reading future passages, make an extra effort to correctly answer the questions in that particular category. Fourth, if the difficulty continues, arrange to see your teacher.

Reading in the Content Areas
SCIENCE

1 Matter

Matter is all around you. Matter is the substance that makes all things. Scientists define matter as anything that has weight and takes up space. Is it possible to prove that the things you see around you are made of matter? Actually, such a proof just requires that you use a little common sense.

First, does each item have weight? Scientists use a scale to prove whether something has weight. A book, for example, might weigh one pound. A person might weigh 125 pounds. A sandwich might weigh only six ounces. If we put any of these items on a scale, we can find how much they weigh. Therefore, each item has a specific weight.

Second, let's prove that the things you see take up space. For example, a book lying on a desk takes up space on the surface of the desk. A person sitting on a chair fills space in the chair. A sandwich in a plastic bag fills space in the bag. Once you know that a book, a person, and a sandwich have weight and take up space, you can see that they all are made of matter.

What about things that you can't see, such as air? Air is difficult to weigh on a scale. But you know that something that is heavy can move lighter things out of its way. Air moves the leaves on plants and the hairs on our head, so we can conclude that air has weight. It's also true that if you blow air into a balloon, the air fills space inside the balloon. Since air has weight and takes up space, it is clear that it is made of matter.

Not everything, however, is made of matter. For example, you might have a million things on your mind. Those things, however, are abstract thoughts and ideas. Thoughts and ideas are items that neither have weight nor take up space. Thus they are not made of matter.

Main Idea 1

	Answer	Score
Mark the *main idea*	M	15
Mark the statement that is *too broad*	B	5
Mark the statement that is *too narrow*	N	5

a. Matter has weight and takes up space.	☐	____
b. Matter is in everything.	☐	____
c. A sandwich is made of matter.	☐	____

Score 15 points for each correct answer.   Score

Subject Matter **2** This passage is mainly about
☐ a. how to show if something is made of matter.
☐ b. how scientists measure the weight of matter.
☐ c. how scientists measure the space of matter.
☐ d. types of matter that we cannot see.   _____

Supporting Details **3** A characteristic of all matter is that it
☐ a. can be seen.
☐ b. occupies the mind.
☐ c. can be eaten.
☐ d. occupies space.   _____

Conclusion **4** The final paragraph suggests that to be sure something is matter, you must
☐ a. evaluate your thoughts and ideas.
☐ b. clear your mind of your worries.
☐ c. prove that it has weight and takes up space.
☐ d. be able to see and touch it.   _____

Clarifying Devices **5** The author orders the ideas in the passage by using
☐ a. a spatial description.
☐ b. time order.
☐ c. cause and effect.
☐ d. signal words such as *first* and *second*.   _____

Vocabulary in Context **6** An example of something <u>abstract</u> is a
☐ a. dream.
☐ b. window.
☐ c. feather.
☐ d. thread.

Add your scores for questions 1–6. Enter the total here   Total
and on the graph on page 158.   Score   _____

2 The Common Cold

Got the sniffles? You're not alone. The common cold will strike in the United States more than 61 million times this year. That's a lot of stuffy noses, sore throats, and coughs. You'd think scientists would have found a cure by now. For being so common, however, a cold is quite complex.

A cold is caused by a virus. And it's not just one type of virus. More than 200 viruses cause colds. A cold virus attacks healthy cells of the nose, throat, or lungs. The virus gets into the cells and takes control. A single virus makes hundreds or thousands of cold viruses inside each cell. Eventually, the cell bursts open and dies. The viruses, though, escape and attack other healthy cells. By now you're sneezing and coughing. Your throat is sore. The viruses keep infecting your healthy cells.

Only your body can fight cold viruses. Billions of white blood cells travel in the blood. White blood cells make <u>antibodies</u>. These proteins attach themselves to viruses and destroy them. It's a slow process. Killing the viruses takes one to two weeks.

What can you do to fight a cold? There isn't much you can do. Antibiotic drugs don't work against viruses. Nose drops and cough medicines only relieve symptoms. Chicken soup seems to help. Vitamin C may help too. A dose of 1,000 milligrams of Vitamin C on the first day of a cold may quicken your recovery.

Be healthy so you don't catch a cold at all. Eat a well-balanced diet and get eight hours of sleep each day. Exercise regularly. Stay away from coughing, sneezing people, because the cold virus spreads through the air. Remember that the cold virus can live up to three hours outside the body. That means you can pick it up from touching money, doorknobs, and other people. So wash your hands often. Prevention is the best action!

Main Idea	1	Answer	Score
	Mark the *main idea*	M	15
	Mark the statement that is *too broad*	B	5
	Mark the statement that is *too narrow*	N	5
	a. A cold is a very common illness.	☐	____
	b. The common cold is caused by a virus that antibodies will finally kill.	☐	____
	c. More than 200 viruses can cause the common cold.	☐	____

Score 15 points for each correct answer.　　　　　　**Score**

Subject Matter　**2**　This passage is mainly concerned with
- ☐ a. antibodies.
- ☐ b. viruses.
- ☐ c. antibiotics.
- ☐ d. common colds.　　　　　　_____

Supporting Details　**3**　The common cold is started by
- ☐ a. a low white-blood cell count.
- ☐ b. a virus.
- ☐ c. a poor diet.
- ☐ d. shaking hands with other people.　　_____

Conclusion　**4**　We can conclude from this passage that the common cold
- ☐ a. will be curable in the near future.
- ☐ b. causes fatigue and watery eyes.
- ☐ c. is something people just have to live with.
- ☐ d. can be prevented with nose drops.　　_____

Clarifying Devices　**5**　In the second and third paragraphs, the author explains the workings of a cold virus through
- ☐ a. a step-by-step explanation.
- ☐ b. scientific studies.
- ☐ c. detailed word pictures.
- ☐ d. a list of symptoms.　　　　　　_____

Vocabulary in Context　**6**　<u>Antibodies</u> are
- ☐ a. proteins that attack viruses.
- ☐ b. white blood cells.
- ☐ c. drugs that fight viruses.
- ☐ d. vitamins.

Add your scores for questions 1–6. Enter the total here and on the graph on page 158.　　**Total Score**　_____

3 Water for Life

Heading out for some exercise? You'll take your shoes, socks, and a towel. You might take a music headset. But you'll also need a water bottle. Here is why. When you exercise, you sweat. Sweating is your body's way of cooling down. The more you sweat, the more water your body loses. But exercise also reduces thirst. If you're not thirsty, you may not drink water. You could lose too much water and become <u>dehydrated</u>. A water loss of 10 percent can make you sick. A water loss of 20 percent can kill you. So you need to be careful.

Here's how to keep your body hydrated. About two hours before you exercise, drink one 500-milliliter ($\frac{1}{2}$ liter) bottle of water. Then drink another half bottle right before you begin. Drink water every 20 minutes as you exercise. You'll need water long before you're thirsty.

You need water even when you're not exercising. You should drink about four bottles of water each day. Why so much? Your body cells are mostly water. So is your blood. Water helps your body to digest food and remove wastes. But your body loses water as you breathe, sweat, and urinate. It loses about 2.5 liters (2,500 milliliters) of water each day.

You must replace the water your body loses. You can get water from many sources. Drinking water is the best source. Food and other fluids are good too. All food has some water in it. Fruits and vegetables are high in water. Milk, juices, and other drinks have water. So take your pick. And remember to drink more water when you exercise. A happy body is a hydrated body!

Main Idea	1		
		Answer	**Score**
	Mark the *main idea*	M	15
	Mark the statement that is *too broad*	B	5
	Mark the statement that is *too narrow*	N	5

a. Your body loses about 2.5 liters of water each day. ☐ _____

b. Your body needs water whether you are exercising or not. ☐ _____

c. Water is important for everyone. ☐ _____

Score 15 points for each correct answer.   **Score**

Subject Matter   2   This passage is mainly about
☐ a. the benefits of a regular workout.
☐ b. sports equipment to take to the gym.
☐ c. why our bodies need water.
☐ d. how many milliliters a water bottle holds.   _____

Supporting Details   3   Losing 10 percent of your body's water
☐ a. will not hurt you during exercise.
☐ b. can make you ill.
☐ c. can kill you.
☐ d. will make your skin feel very cold.   _____

Conclusion   4   Each day you should drink
☐ a. about 2,500 milliliters of water.
☐ b. about 500 milliliters of water.
☐ c. as much milk as you can.
☐ d. only when you get thirsty.   _____

Clarifying Devices   5   The author tells how to keep your body hydrated during exercise by presenting
☐ a. a diagram.
☐ b. a description of a human blood vessel.
☐ c. a series of steps to follow.
☐ d. the results of an experiment.   _____

Vocabulary in Context   6   To become dehydrated is to
☐ a. drink too much water.
☐ b. lose more water than you take in.
☐ c. exercise at least four days a week.
☐ d. cool off after exercising.

Add your scores for questions 1–6. Enter the total here and on the graph on page 158.   **Total Score**   _____

7

4 Brain Cells

What are you doing right now? Yes, you are reading this page. That also means you're moving your eyes. You're thinking. You're breathing. You're listening. Possibly you're shifting positions. You're feeling things such as this book. You're also feeling emotions. What lets you do all these things at the same time? You're brain.

· Your brain is the control center of your body and mind. Without your brain, you could not do anything. Your brain contains more than 100 billion nerve cells. Each nerve cell makes from 1,000 to 10,000 connections with other nerve cells. The nerve cells send <u>impulses</u> back and forth within your brain and to and from every part of your body. After you reach the age of 20, though, your brain cells start to die. This is normal. However, if you suffer a stroke, an illness, or an injury, even more nerve cells die in your brain. When a nerve cell dies, the thousands of connections it made with other nerve cells are lost.

Until recently, scientists believed that the brain did not replace its dead cells. New studies, however, prove otherwise. Scientists have found new nerve cells in a part of the brain called the hippocampus. The hippocampus helps the brain form memories from new experiences.

The discovery of these new nerve cells is not a cure for anything yet. It gives hope, however, of a cure for brain damage caused by epilepsy, Lou Gehrig's disease, car accidents, and strokes. Someday scientists might be able to use the new cells to replace damaged brain cells. Such a cure, however, may take decades to develop. So in the meantime, use your head—protect it!

Main Idea	1		Answer	Score
	Mark the *main idea*		M	15
	Mark the statement that is *too broad*		B	5
	Mark the statement that is *too narrow*		N	5

a. Nerve cells in the brain begin to die when a person reaches the age of 20. ☐ _____

b. There are a lot of things going on in the human brain. ☐ _____

c. The brain is a control center regulating thoughts, feelings, and actions. ☐ _____

Subject Matter   2   This passage is mainly about
    ☐ a. why people should wear bike helmets.
    ☐ b. the number of activities humans can do
        at the same time.
    ☐ c. the importance of nerve cells in the brain.
    ☐ d. the number of connections made between
        nerve cells.   _____

**Supporting
Details**   3   Nerve cells in the brain
    ☐ a. send messages to every part of the body.
    ☐ b. make connections only to other cells in
        the brain.
    ☐ c. can cure Lou Gehrig's disease.
    ☐ d. are a person's memory.   _____

Conclusion   4   The last sentence of the passage suggests that people
    ☐ a. should use their heads by carefully thinking
        through situations.
    ☐ b. should be careful not to injure their brains.
    ☐ c. have a skull that provides all the protection
        needed by the brain.
    ☐ d. should see a quick cure for brain disorders.   _____

**Clarifying
Devices**   5   The author makes clear what the hippocampus is by
    ☐ a. tracing its history.
    ☐ b. comparing it to other parts of the brain.
    ☐ c. telling how it got its name.
    ☐ d. explaining what it does.   _____

**Vocabulary
in Context**   6   Nerve <u>impulses</u> are
    ☐ a. cures.
    ☐ b. disorders.
    ☐ c. memories.
    ☐ d. messages.   _____

**Add your scores for questions 1–6. Enter the total here
and on the graph on page 158.**   **Total
Score**   _____

5 Sea Turtles

Watch where you're walking on the beach. You just might step on a sea turtle nest! Sea turtles are reptiles. They have dry, tough skin and breathe air through lungs. Sea turtles eat or sleep in the ocean. When the female is ready for nesting, she swims to shore. She does this at night, after the hot sun has disappeared. She uses her flippers to drag her heavy body slowly through the sand. When she gets to an area above the high-tide line, she stops. Now she puts her rear flippers to work. She digs a hole one to four feet deep where she lays 50 to 100 eggs. She covers and hides the eggs with sand. Finally, she drags herself back to the ocean, never visiting her nest again.

Back in the nest, the eggs <u>incubate</u> under the warmth of the sun and sand. About two months later, the eggs begin to hatch. The baby turtles are about two inches long and weigh only three-fifths of an ounce. The baby turtles dig their way upward. Under cover of night, they run together toward the reflective brightness of the ocean. Many of the young turtles live in the seaweed in the ocean currents for a few years. Later they move into coastal waters. Only one or two out of about 1,000 young turtles live to adulthood.

There are seven species of sea turtles. The smallest is the ridley. An adult ridley weighs 75 to 100 pounds. The biggest is the leatherback. An adult leatherback weighs about 1,300 pounds, and it is almost eight feet long.

Sea turtles live in all the oceans except the coldest ones. They nest only in hot tropical and sub-tropical areas. Their powerful oversized arms let them swim great distances. Some swim hundreds or thousands of miles to feed or nest. Sea turtles don't have teeth. But they have hard, rough jaws that are good for crushing and tearing food. An adult sea turtle lives for 40 to 60 years—much longer than most other animals.

Main Idea	1			
			Answer	Score
	Mark the *main idea*		M	15
	Mark the statement that is *too broad*		B	5
	Mark the statement that is *too narrow*		N	5

a. Sea turtles spend much time in the sea but lay their eggs on shore. ☐ _____

b. A female sea turtle lays 50 to 100 eggs. ☐ _____

c. Sea turtles are long-living animals. ☐ _____

Score 15 points for each correct answer.   Score

Subject Matter 2 Another good title for this passage would be
- [ ] a. Turtle Watching.
- [ ] b. The Littlest Turtles.
- [ ] c. Sun: A Natural Incubator.
- [ ] d. The Life of a Sea Turtle.

_____

Supporting Details 3 Sea turtles have powerful arms so they can
- [ ] a. lay their eggs.
- [ ] b. fight off sharks and whales.
- [ ] c. swim for thousands of miles.
- [ ] d. float in the ocean currents.

_____

Conclusion 4 What conclusion can you draw from this passage?
- [ ] a. Female sea turtles lay their eggs on shore to hide and protect them.
- [ ] b. Sea turtles are learning to dig deeper nests to protect their eggs.
- [ ] c. Baby sea turtles are afraid to go anywhere without their mothers.
- [ ] d. Sea turtles usually travel in pairs.

_____

Clarifying Devices 5 The author develops ideas in the first paragraph by
- [ ] a. comparing and contrasting.
- [ ] b. using signal and transitional words.
- [ ] c. presenting causes and effects.
- [ ] d. order of importance.

_____

Vocabulary in Context 6 In this passage, the word <u>incubate</u> means
- [ ] a. get ready to hatch.
- [ ] b. drown.
- [ ] c. swim.
- [ ] d. come close to dying.

Add your scores for questions 1–6. Enter the total here and on the graph on page 158.   Total Score

_____

6 Fossils

Scientists know much about the earth's history. They estimate that plants and animals lived as long as 3.5 billion years ago. Relatives of some modern animals lived 580 million years ago. Dinosaurs lived about 200 million years ago. The first humans came along about 3.7 million years ago. How do scientists know all this? They find clues in the earth's rocks. Rocks often contain fossils, the preserved remains of things that lived long ago.

Most fossils are the hard parts of living things. Animal bones, teeth, and shells may be fossils. Fossils of plant parts are rare. Plants don't have hard parts. But plant imprints and animal tracks in hardened mud are fossils. Sometimes fossils are whole animals. For example, whole woolly mammoths have been found. They became trapped when glaciers of ice moved across the earth.

Most fossils are found in sedimentary rock. Why? Dead plants and animals fell into lakes and oceans. Sediment, such as sand or mud, covered them. Over time, many layers of sediments collected. The upper layers pushed down on the lower layers. The sediment in the lower layers changed into rock. Bones, teeth, and shells became fossils in the rock. Sometimes a dead animal's body decayed. The body left its shape in the rock. This space is a type of fossil called a mold. Sediments may seep into a mold and harden. This type of fossil is called a cast.

Fossils of ocean animals have been found on mountains. How did they get there? The earth's <u>crust</u> is always moving. The sedimentary rock in lakes and oceans moves with it. That's why fossils of ocean plants and animals can be found on land.

Main Idea	1		Answer	Score
	Mark the *main idea*		M	15
	Mark the statement that is *too broad*		B	5
	Mark the statement that is *too narrow*		N	5

a. Fossils are clues to what long-ago animals and plants looked like. ☐ _____

b. Scientists know much about the earth's history. ☐ _____

c. Fossils of whole woolly mammoths have been found. ☐ _____

Score 15 points for each correct answer.   **Score**

Subject Matter   **2**   This passage is mostly concerned with
- ☐ a. woolly mammoths.
- ☐ b. sedimentary rock.
- ☐ c. fossils.
- ☐ d. ocean animals.   _____

Supporting Details   **3**   Which of the following is **not** a type of fossil?
- ☐ a. a plant imprint
- ☐ b. a mold
- ☐ c. an animal's shell
- ☐ d. a sediment   _____

Conclusion   **4**   We can conclude from this passage that scientists have
- ☐ a. made fossils out of sand and mud.
- ☐ b. studied fossils of ancient plants and animals.
- ☐ c. melted glaciers of ice.
- ☐ d. created dinosaurs in the laboratory.   _____

Clarifying Devices   **5**   The author begins this passage by giving
- ☐ a. facts about life long ago.
- ☐ b. examples of fossils.
- ☐ c. descriptions of glaciers.
- ☐ d. a step-by-step explanation.   _____

Vocabulary in Context   **6**   In this passage, the word <u>crust</u> means
- ☐ a. water.
- ☐ b. part of a piece of bread.
- ☐ c. having a lot of nerve.
- ☐ d. hard outer layer.

Add your scores for questions 1–6. Enter the total here and on the graph on page 158.   **Total Score**   _____

7 Lightning

A flash of bright light zigzags from a cloud. A crash of thunder echoes seconds later. Lightning and thunder make most people jumpy. In early America, Benjamin Franklin linked lightning to science. During a thunderstorm, he flew a kite. He tied a key to the end of the string. Franklin saw sparks jump from the key. He thought the sky was electrically charged. The electric charges went down the string to the key. His work was <u>crucial</u> to understanding lightning. He learned that lightning is an electrical current.

Today we know more. Lightning forms in clouds. A cloud has charged energy in it. The energy at the top of a cloud is positive. The energy at the bottom is negative. Opposites attract. So the positive and negative charges move toward each other. When they meet, they make an electric current. The current forms a bolt of lightning. The bolt moves from the bottom of the cloud. It has a negative charge. We can't see the bolt, but it reaches downward. Positive energy from the ground moves up. When the opposite charges meet, a powerful electric current flows between them. That causes a flash of lightning. Its temperature is about 50,000 degrees Fahrenheit. That's almost five times hotter than the surface of the sun! The lightning heats the air around it. The heated air quickly expands. As it moves, it causes a shock wave. That's the thunder we hear.

Lightning kills about 200 people in the United States each year. It injures about 700 people. These tips can help you be safe. When lightning strikes, don't stand under a tree. Stay away from metal objects. Get out of and away from pools and lakes. Move into a building or get inside a car. Indoors, stay away from windows and doors. Unplug electrical appliances. Stay off the telephone. Seek immediate medical attention for anyone struck by lightning. Remember, lightning kills. So play it safe!

Main Idea   1

	Answer	Score
Mark the *main idea*	M	15
Mark the statement that is *too broad*	B	5
Mark the statement that is *too narrow*	N	5

a. Lightning kills about 200 people in the United States each year. ☐ _____

b. Lightning and thunder are weather events. ☐ _____

c. Lightning is a dangerous electric current between clouds and the earth. ☐ _____

Subject Matter   **2**   This passage is mainly about
- ☐ a. similarities between thunder and lightning.
- ☐ b. why Ben Franklin flew a kite in a storm.
- ☐ c. what lightning is and how to be safe from it.
- ☐ d. why the temperature of lightning is greater than the temperature of the sun.   _____

Supporting Details   **3**   A lightning bolt results when
- ☐ a. the temperature reaches 50,000 degrees Fahrenheit.
- ☐ b. negative and positive energy come together.
- ☐ c. a key is attached to a kite.
- ☐ d. people stand under a tree during a storm.   _____

Conclusion   **4**   The sentence "opposites attract" suggests that negatively charged energy
- ☐ a. is attracted to thunder.
- ☐ b. forms a lightning bolt.
- ☐ c. quickly heats the air around it.
- ☐ d. will move toward positively charged energy.   _____

Clarifying Devices   **5**   The first two sentences of this passage
- ☐ a. are exaggerations.
- ☐ b. help you imagine a thunderstorm.
- ☐ c. take you back into United States history.
- ☐ d. explain the meaning of the word _jumpy._   _____

Vocabulary in Context   **6**   The word <u>crucial</u> means
- ☐ a. extremely wet.
- ☐ b. not meaningful.
- ☐ c. very important.
- ☐ d. dark and stormy.

Add your scores for questions 1–6. Enter the total here and on the graph on page 158.   Total Score   _____

8 Identifying the *Danaus plexippus*

This creature is found anywhere in the world where it's not too hot or too cold. It has six legs and four orange-and-black wings. Its color suggested its name: King William of Holland was the Prince of Orange—the future monarch of England. The creature is a daytime traveler but only in good conditions. It takes shelter during rainstorms. When it flies, it flutters. It glides and soars through the air. Airplane pilots have spotted it as high as three-quarters of a mile above the earth. Its speed of 12 miles per hour isn't as fast as a bird's. It's impressive, though, since this creature weighs only seven ounces. It goes the distance too. It may cover 80 miles in one day. Long trips of 1,500 miles are common in late summer. For energy, it sips nectar from flowers. At the same time it carries pollen from plant to plant. This helps the plants produce more seeds, which become plants. Have you figured out what this amazing insect is? Its scientific name is *Danaus plexippus,* but it's better known as the monarch butterfly.

Monarchs can live up to nine months, though most live only two to five weeks. Females are very busy during that time. They lay about 700 eggs, one egg at a time. Each egg is laid on a different milkweed plant. When the egg hatches, a caterpillar comes out. It is an "eating machine." It eats its shell. It eats the milkweed plant on which it was laid. Eating is about all it does until it is fully grown. Then it attaches itself to a twig. The caterpillar forms a <u>chrysalis</u> around itself. Like a moth's cocoon, a chrysalis protects the caterpillar. Inside the chrysalis, the caterpillar changes into a butterfly. Next the butterfly splits open the chrysalis and crawls out. It hangs onto the chrysalis for about two hours until its wings dry. The change from egg to caterpillar to chrysalis to butterfly takes three to four weeks. Finally the monarch is ready to fly.

Main Idea	1		Answer	Score
	Mark the *main idea*		M	15
	Mark the statement that is *too broad*		B	5
	Mark the statement that is *too narrow*		N	5

a. The monarch butterfly was named after King William, the Prince of Orange. ☐ _____

b. The high-flying monarch goes through several changes from egg to butterfly. ☐ _____

c. Monarchs are a type of butterfly. ☐ _____

Score 15 points for each correct answer.   **Score**

Subject Matter	**2**	Another good title for this passage would be

☐ a. Butterflies.
☐ b. A Nectar Drinker.
☐ c. Cocoon.
☐ d. The Ramarkable Monarch.   _____

Supporting Details   **3**   Which of the following shows the order in which a butterfly develops?

☐ a. butterfly to egg to caterpillar to chrysalis
☐ b. butterfly to egg to chrysalis to caterpillar
☐ c. egg to caterpillar to chrysalis to butterfly
☐ d. egg to chrysalis to caterpillar to butterfly   _____

Conclusion   **4**   We can conclude from this passage that monarchs

☐ a. eat a lot of plants but also help plants to reproduce.
☐ b. are the world's largest butterflies.
☐ c. need a scientific name that is more descriptive.
☐ d. have trouble flying at high altitudes.   _____

Clarifying Devices   **5**   The author explains the phrase "eating Machine" by presenting

☐ a. a strong argument.
☐ b. examples.
☐ c. precise measurements.
☐ d. a scientific study.   _____

Vocabulary in Context   **6**   A chrysalis is a

☐ a. crystal.
☐ b. stem for caterpillars to crawl on.
☐ c. protective shelter for a caterpillar.
☐ d. monarch butterfly.   _____

Add your scores for questions 1–6. Enter the total here and on the graph on page 158.   **Total Score**   _____

9 Sleep

Are you tired? Do you feel grouchy and less alert than usual? Do you often catch colds and flu? If so, you might consider changing your sleep habits. Good health demands good sleep. Studies have shown that most people need eight hours of sleep each day. Americans, however, on the average get only seven hours. One-third of us get just six hours. And good health is not simply a matter of how much sleep you get. It's also the type of sleep.

Non-rapid eye movement (NREM) sleep lets your body grow and repair itself. During NREM sleep, your muscles relax. Your heart rate and breathing rate decrease. Your eyes roll slowly back and forth; then they stop moving. Most of the sleeping you do is NREM sleep.

Rapid eye movement (REM) sleep restores your brain. During REM sleep, you dream. You may not remember every dream. But every time you sleep, you dream. Your eyes move back and forth quickly. Your breathing and heartbeat increase. Your muscles become paralyzed. About 25 percent of your sleep is REM sleep. You need enough of both kinds of sleep to be healthy.

Is it a real concern if you don't get enough good sleep? It certainly is. Poor sleep puts you and others at risk. More than 100,000 car accidents are caused each year by drivers who nod off. Almost $100 billion is lost yearly in the business and environmental sectors. People <u>deprived</u> of sleep have been factors in the *Challenger* space shuttle tragedy, the Exxon *Valdez* oil spill, and the Chernobyl nuclear reactor accident. So do yourself and everyone around you a favor. Don't cheat yourself out of good sleep!

Main Idea	1		Answer	Score
	Mark the *main idea*		M	15
	Mark the statement that is *too broad*		B	5
	Mark the statement that is *too narrow*		N	5

a. People don't get enough sleep. ☐ _____

b. We dream during REM sleep. ☐ _____

c. Everyone needs good sleep to be
physically and mentally healthy. ☐ _____

Score 15 points for each correct answer.   **Score**

Subject Matter **2** This passage is mainly about why
- ☐ a. people dream.
- ☐ b. muscles become paralyzed during sleep.
- ☐ c. people catch colds and the flu.
- ☐ d. people need good sleep.   _____

Supporting Details **3** Most nightly sleep is
- ☐ a. NREM sleep.
- ☐ b. REM sleep.
- ☐ c. sleep occurring between 1:00 and 3:00 A.M.
- ☐ d. sleep that restores your brain.   _____

Conclusion **4** "Good sleep" can be described as
- ☐ a. about eight hours of NREM and REM sleep.
- ☐ b. sleeping soundly when you're sick.
- ☐ c. several hours of rest each day.
- ☐ d. the time in which you dream.   _____

Clarifying Devices **5** To help the reader understand how business and the environment are affected by poor sleep habits, the writer
- ☐ a. lists facts in time order.
- ☐ b. compares and contrasts two accidents.
- ☐ c. lists several big accidents.
- ☐ d. uses transition words.   _____

Vocabulary in Context **6** In this passage, <u>deprived</u> means
- ☐ a. permitted to.
- ☐ b. kept from having.
- ☐ c. enjoying.
- ☐ d. wishing to.   _____

Add your scores for questions 1–6. Enter the total here and on the graph on page 158.   **Total Score**   _____

10 Seed Plants

What plants do you see in your neighborhood? Trees such as maple and ginkgo and flowers such as geraniums and columbines are possibilities. Fruits and crops such as strawberries, pumpkins, and corn may grow in some gardens. You're also likely to see grass and weeds. All these plants, and most others we see, are seed plants. Seed plants—plants grown from seeds—need water, sunlight, and minerals to thrive.

All seed plants have three main parts: roots, stems, and leaves; some seed plants also have flowers. Each part of a plant is essential for its continuing development. Roots grow downward into the soil or toward water. As the roots branch out throughout the soil, they <u>absorb</u> water and minerals. The roots of some plants also store food to help the plants survive the winter. Roots act as an anchor, holding the plant firmly in the soil.

Most stems grow above ground. Some seed plants, however, have special stems that grow underground. For example, onions and tulips have bulbs, which are stem parts that grow underground. Stems have tubes that carry food, water, and minerals throughout the plant. Stems also grow leaves and hold them up toward sunlight. Green plants use energy from the sun to make food through photosynthesis, which takes place in the leaves and sometimes in the stems of seed plants.

Seed plants form seeds to reproduce new plants. Some form seeds, such as pine cones and acorns, on branches of leaves. Other plants, such as apples and cucumbers, have flowers that make seeds inside the fruit. The seeds of all plants grow into new plants, many of which play important roles in our lives. Wood, rubber, dyes, medicines, cloth fibers, and cooking oils all come from seed plants. Most importantly, we depend on seed plants as sources of food for animals and for ourselves.

Main Idea	1		Answer	Score
	Mark the *main idea*		M	15
	Mark the statement that is *too broad*		B	5
	Mark the statement that is *too narrow*		N	5
	a. Most plants are seed plants.		☐	_____
	b. Some seed plants have flowers as well as roots, stems, and leaves.		☐	_____
	c. Seed plants have many parts and can serve many purposes.		☐	_____

Score 15 points for each correct answer.   **Score**

Subject Matter   **2**   The purpose of this passage is to
☐ a. give a history of seed plants.
☐ b. describe the parts of seed plants and their purposes.
☐ c. compare seed plants and seedless plants.
☐ d. describe several uses of seed plants.   _____

Supporting Details   **3**   The roots of a seed plant
☐ a. hold the plant in the ground.
☐ b. grow above ground and develop leaves.
☐ c. are important for photosynthesis.
☐ d. reproduce new plants by forming seeds.   _____

Conclusion   **4**   After reading this passage, we can conclude that
☐ a. seed plants do not need seeds to reproduce.
☐ b. green plants will thrive in areas with little sunlight and water.
☐ c. photosynthesis happens only at night.
☐ d. human life is dependent on seed plants.   _____

Clarifying Devices   **5**   To make the point that some seed plants have special stems that grow underground, the author
☐ a. describes places where these plants grow.
☐ b. tells some uses of seed plants.
☐ c. uses the example of plants with bulbs.
☐ d. uses the example of flowers that make seeds inside a fruit.   _____

Vocabulary in Context   **6**   To <u>absorb</u> means to
☐ a. grow and live.
☐ b. suck up and take in.
☐ c. want and need.
☐ d. carry and use.   _____

Add your scores for questions 1–6. Enter the total here and on the graph on page 158.   **Total Score**   _____

11 Lights in the Night Sky

Look into the sky on a clear night, away from city lights. What do you see? Your eyes are dazzled by thousands of points of lights. Some of the lights twinkle; others glow steadily. The twinkling points of lights are stars, or large balls of very hot gases such as hydrogen, helium, iron, and calcium. The gases cause nuclear reactions inside the stars. The nuclear reactions release energy in the forms of light and heat. On a clear night, you can see as many as 2,500 stars with the naked eye. The points of light that have a steady glow are planets, most likely Venus, Mars, Jupiter, or Saturn. The difference between stars and planets in the sky is that stars give off their own light. The brightness of planets is caused by light reflected from the sun.

Some stars are <u>isolated</u> in the sky; others are grouped into clusters. Stars and star clusters are grouped into even larger groups called galaxies. There are tens of millions of galaxies in the universe. Our galaxy, the Milky Way, contains more than 100 billion stars. The universe contains more than a billion billion stars. Each star has its own position in space. That's why we know where to look in the sky for individual stars, such as Polaris, and for arrangements of stars, such as the Big Dipper.

Though stars look small, they actually are quite large. A star can range in size from thousands to millions of miles across. Most stars only look small because they are so far away from Earth. Distance also plays a role in a star's brightness when viewed from Earth. The larger and hotter the star, the brighter it is. But two stars of the same size and temperature will not appear to have the same brightness if they are at different distances from Earth. The star farther away from Earth will seem dimmer than the one that is closer. The very closest star to Earth is the sun.

Main Idea	1		Answer	Score
	Mark the *main idea*		M	15
	Mark the statement that is *too broad*		B	5
	Mark the statement that is *too narrow*		N	5

a. Stars, huge balls of hot gases, can be found by the billions in our universe. ☐ _____

b. There are thousands of bright lights in the night sky. ☐ _____

c. Every star has its own particular position in the sky. ☐ _____

Subject Matter   **2**   This passage is mostly concerned with
- ☐ a. stars.
- ☐ b. light energy.
- ☐ c. galaxies.
- ☐ d. planets.   _____

Supporting Details   **3**   The Milky Way is a
- ☐ a. star.
- ☐ b. universe.
- ☐ c. galaxy.
- ☐ d. star cluster.   _____

Conclusion   **4**   The author's conclusion that the sun is Earth's nearest star is
- ☐ a. incorrect because the sun is a planet similar to Earth.
- ☐ b. correct because authors never mislead their readers.
- ☐ c. incorrect because no star is as hot as the sun.
- ☐ d. correct because the sun gives off light and heat and is the largest visible point of light.   _____

Clarifying Devices   **5**   The first paragraph of this passage does **not** include
- ☐ a. a definition of a star.
- ☐ b. the names of several bodies in the night sky.
- ☐ c. facts about the size of stars.
- ☐ d. a comparison between stars and planets.   _____

Vocabulary in Context   **6**   To be <u>isolated</u> means to be
- ☐ a. together in a group.
- ☐ b. set apart from others.
- ☐ c. twinkling and sparkling.
- ☐ d. in a set position in space.   _____

Add your scores for questions 1–6. Enter the total here and on the graph on page 158.   **Total Score**   _____

12 The Basics of Weather

The alarm clock rings. You turn on the radio to hear the weather report. Why? Weather affects everything in our lives. It affects what we wear and the activities we perform. It affects the crops we grow and the work we do. But what *is* weather? It is what's happening in the atmosphere, that thick layer of air that surrounds the earth. Air temperature, wind, precipitation, and clouds work together to create weather.

The sun has a great effect on weather. Why? The sun warms the surface of the earth. Some parts of land warm faster than others. A parking lot, for instance, absorbs the sun's heat more quickly than a forest. All land, however, absorbs the sun's heat faster than a body of water. A forest, therefore, warms more quickly than a large lake or ocean. The warmed land and water give off heat to the air above them. The hot air rises, and as it <u>ascends,</u> cooler air moves in to replace it. This movement of air is called wind.

The sun's heat also causes water from land, oceans, and lakes to evaporate into the air. Other water vapor, or gas, is released into the air from plants, animals, and people. As water vapor rises in the air, it cools and forms drops of water. The drops of water form clouds. Inside a cloud, the drops join together, becoming larger and larger. When they get too big and heavy, they fall as precipitation. Rain is the most common form of precipitation. But when the air in and below a cloud is cold enough, the precipitation may fall as sleet, hail, or snow.

Clouds affect air temperature as well as precipitation. Clouds keep some of the sun's heat from reaching the earth. On a mostly cloudy day, less of the sun's heat reaches the earth. So when the weather report predicts a mostly cloudy day, consider dressing a tad warmer.

Main Idea	1		
		Answer	Score
	Mark the *main idea*	M	15
	Mark the statement that is *too broad*	B	5
	Mark the statement that is *too narrow*	N	5
	a. Hot air rises.	☐	_____
	b. Weather is in the atmosphere.	☐	_____
	c. Temperature, wind, precipitation, and clouds work together to create weather.	☐	_____

Subject Matter 2 Another good title for this passage is
- [ ] a. Weather: A Combination of Factors.
- [ ] b. Radio and the Weather.
- [ ] c. Keep That Sweater Handy.
- [ ] d. Weather Extremes: Why They Happen. ____

Supporting Details 3 The most important fact about the sun in this passage is that it
- [ ] a. is the center of our universe.
- [ ] b. radiates sunshine to all the planets and stars.
- [ ] c. warms the earth and causes water to evaporate.
- [ ] d. hides behind clouds in the sky. ____

Conclusion 4 It is clear that
- [ ] a. early risers listen to weather reports.
- [ ] b. precipitation makes clouds in the sky.
- [ ] c. weather forecasters should be more accurate.
- [ ] d. weather would not happen if the sun were cold. ____

Clarifying Devices 5 To help show that surfaces absorb heat at different rates, the author uses
- [ ] a. strong arguments.
- [ ] b. a brief story.
- [ ] c. examples.
- [ ] d. measurements. ____

Vocabulary in Context 6 Ascends means
- [ ] a. goes down.
- [ ] b. goes up.
- [ ] c. goes from north to south.
- [ ] d. goes in a circle. ____

Add your scores for questions 1–6. Enter the total here and on the graph on page 158. **Total Score** ____

13 Forces and Motion

Our lives are in constant motion. We move ourselves by walking, driving, or riding. We move food and goods in trucks, ships, airplanes, and trains. We move parts and products using pulleys and conveyor belts. We move satellites into space with rockets. All the ways we move things are based on a simple <u>principle</u>. A push or a pull can make things move. A push or a pull can also change an object's direction and speed. A push or a pull is a force, and forces control the motion of objects.

Anytime you see an object move or stop moving, a force is acting on the object. For example, when you hit a hockey puck on ice, the puck speeds up. It slides across the ice for a distance. Then it slows down and stops moving. The force that causes the puck to slow down and stop is friction. Without friction, the puck would keep moving. Friction is the force between two surfaces that acts in the opposite direction of the motion. The amount of friction depends on how tightly the two surfaces are pressed together and how slick they are. Very slick surfaces, such as ice and waxed floors, create less friction than rough surfaces.

Earth's gravity affects the motion of objects too. Gravity is the force that pulls things toward the earth's surface. Consider a ball's motion when you throw it horizontally. The ball moves in the direction you threw it. The force of gravity, however, pulls down on the ball, giving it a curved path until the ball strikes the ground. Without gravity, the ball would keep moving in the direction you threw it.

We have put our understanding of forces into machines and technology. As a result, we have electrical, magnetic, aerodynamic, and other forces. These forces control motion in our homes, cities, skies, waterways, and beyond.

Main Idea	1	Answer	Score
	Mark the *main idea*	M	15
	Mark the statement that is *too broad*	B	5
	Mark the statement that is *too narrow*	N	5
	a. Gravity pulls objects toward the earth.	☐	_____
	b. Things on the earth are always moving.	☐	_____
	c. Forces control when and how objects move.	☐	_____

Subject Matter **2** The purpose of this passage is to
- ☐ a. explain how friction and gravity control motion.
- ☐ b. describe how we transport goods.
- ☐ c. keep people from falling on ice.
- ☐ d. compare pushes and pulls. _____

Supporting Details **3** Without friction and gravity, moving objects would
- ☐ a. go around in circles.
- ☐ b. slow down and eventually stop.
- ☐ c. be pulled down to the earth.
- ☐ d. keep moving in the same direction. _____

Conclusion **4** We can conclude from the second paragraph that
- ☐ a. hockey pucks slide on their own.
- ☐ b. an empty box could be pushed more easily across a floor than a box of books.
- ☐ c. there is no friction on ice.
- ☐ d. rough surfaces create less friction than slick surfaces do. _____

Clarifying Devices **5** To explain gravity, the author uses the example of a
- ☐ a. conveyor belt.
- ☐ b. ball that's been thrown.
- ☐ c. hockey puck.
- ☐ d. satellite. _____

Vocabulary in Context **6** In this passage, <u>principle</u> means
- ☐ a. rule or law.
- ☐ b. head of a school.
- ☐ c. a belief that helps people be good.
- ☐ d. vision. _____

Add your scores for questions 1–6. Enter the total here and on the graph on page 158.   **Total Score** _____

14 A Balanced Diet

Your body works 24 hours a day. It's always building and repairing, feeding and cleansing itself. Its goal is to be ready for your every movement, breath, and thought. The quality of your life depends on how well your body works. And how well your body works depends on how much energy it gets. Energy comes from the food you eat. Food contains <u>nutrients</u> that your body needs for growth and energy.

By eating a balanced diet, your body gets the six essential nutrients it needs. *Minerals* are nutrients that build bones and teeth. Minerals also form red blood cells and other substances. *Water* aids digestion and waste removal. *Carbohydrates* give your body its main source of energy. Two carbohydrates are sugars from foods such as fruits and vegetables and starches found in rice, potatoes, and bread. *Fats* help build cell membranes. *Proteins* repair and grow body tissues. Finally, *vitamins* help your body use carbohydrates, fats, and proteins.

The United States Department of Agriculture (USDA) has created a nutritional food pyramid. It shows the daily number of servings you should eat from five food groups. The food pyramid has four levels. The base of the pyramid is the largest level. It contains the bread, cereal, rice, and pasta group from which you need six to eleven servings. The next level has two food groups: vegetables and fruits. The USDA recommends three to five servings of vegetables and two to four servings of fruit. The third level also has two groups: the milk, yogurt, and cheese group and the meat, poultry, fish, dry beans, eggs, and nuts group. You need two to three servings from each of these groups. The top of the pyramid is the smallest level. It contains fats, oils, and sweets. These foods have few nutrients, so eat them sparingly.

Main Idea	1		
		Answer	Score
Mark the *main idea*		M	15
Mark the statement that is *too broad*		B	5
Mark the statement that is *too narrow*		N	5

a. Eating a balanced diet gives your body the energy it needs. ☐ _____

b. A balanced diet is important for everyone. ☐ _____

c. Meat, poultry, fish, dry beans, eggs, and nuts are on the third level. ☐ _____

Subject Matter   **2**   Another good title for this passage is

     ☐ a. What You Need to Know About Fats.

     ☐ b. An Apple a Day Keeps the Doctor Away.

     ☐ c. Water: An Essential Nutrient.

     ☐ d. Eating for Life and Health.   _____

Supporting   **3**   A balanced diet
Details

     ☐ a. consists of foods from five food groups.

     ☐ b. includes many foods containing fat.

     ☐ c. includes six to eleven servings of fruit.

     ☐ d. can be obtained by taking vitamins.   _____

Conclusion   **4**   The first paragraph suggests that food

     ☐ a. is something that cleanses your body.

     ☐ b. can improve the quality of your life.

     ☐ c. should be eaten at night as well as during the day.

     ☐ d. will make it easier for you to exercise.   _____

Clarifying   **5**   To help the reader identify the six nutrients
Devices   needed by the body, the author

     ☐ a. describes the five basic food groups.

     ☐ b. explains what a balanced diet is.

     ☐ c. writes the name of each nutrient in italics.

     ☐ d. tells the number of daily servings needed from each food group.   _____

Vocabulary   **6**   A <u>nutrient</u> is
in Context

     ☐ a. a substance that gives the body energy.

     ☐ b. a type of blood cell.

     ☐ c. a body tissue.

     ☐ d. the quality of your life.   _____

Add your scores for questions 1–6. Enter the total here   **Total**
and on the graph on page 158.   **Score**   _____

15 Eclipses

It's a bright sunny day. Suddenly the day turns dark, and stars come out. A few minutes later, bright sunlight returns. What has happened? Maybe heavenly monsters injured or killed the sun. Perhaps the sun fainted or got sick. Maybe it lost a battle with the moon. These are only some of the beliefs of ancient peoples around the world. People developed ceremonies and rituals to chase away the monsters and to honor and calm the sun and the moon. Today, most people are aware of a scientific explanation: the moon eclipsed the sun, or moved in front of it.

Eclipses occur only on rare occasions when the sun, moon, and Earth are in a straight line. A solar eclipse occurs when the moon moves between the sun and Earth. The bright sun casts the moon's shadow on part of Earth. The shadow has two parts: the umbra and the penumbra. Areas on Earth in the moon's umbra, or the shadow's center, experience a total solar eclipse. In these areas, the entire sun is hidden behind the moon. In some areas, the eclipse may last as long as 7.5 minutes.

Areas on Earth in the moon's penumbra, or the part of the shadow outside the umbra, experience a partial solar eclipse. In these areas, only part of the sun is <u>obscured</u>. The moon's penumbra covers a larger area on Earth than the umbra does. So more areas on Earth experience partial solar eclipses than total solar eclipses.

A lunar eclipse occurs when Earth moves between the sun and the moon. The sun casts Earth's shadow on the moon. Similar to the moon's shadow, Earth's shadow has a central umbra surrounded by a penumbra. If the moon is in Earth's umbra, a total lunar eclipse occurs, and the whole moon darkens. If the moon is in Earth's penumbra, a partial lunar eclipse occurs. Only part of the moon darkens. People anywhere on Earth can see a lunar eclipse that occurs at normal moonlight times.

Main Idea	1		
		Answer	Score
	Mark the *main idea*	M	15
	Mark the statement that is *too broad*	B	5
	Mark the statement that is *too narrow*	N	5

a. Some ancient people believed that a solar eclipse occurred when the moon destroyed the sun in battle. ☐ _____

b. Eclipses are a phenomenon of nature. ☐ _____

c. Eclipses occur when the sun casts shadows on the moon or Earth. ☐ _____

Score 15 points for each correct answer.　　　　　　　**Score**

Subject Matter　**2**　Another good title for this passage is

☐ a. Heavenly Bodies in Battle.

☐ b. Beliefs and Facts About Eclipses.

☐ c. Totally Eclipsed Inside the Umbra.

☐ d. Bright Lights and Dark Shadows.　　　_____

Supporting Details　**3**　An eclipse occurs when

☐ a. people see the moon darken.

☐ b. the sun gets very bright.

☐ c. monsters in the sky try to kill the sun or moon.

☐ d. the sun, moon, and Earth are in a line.　　　_____

Conclusion　**4**　We can conclude from this passage that

☐ a. ancient people feared eclipses.

☐ b. ancient people understood eclipses.

☐ c. many people today fear eclipses.

☐ d. eclipses occur about once a month.　　　_____

Clarifying Devices　**5**　To show that the moon's shadow determines whether a solar eclipse is total or partial, the author

☐ a. discusses the beliefs of ancient peoples.

☐ b. tells how long a solar eclipse may last.

☐ c. describes the two parts of the shadow.

☐ d. tells how often solar eclipses occur.　　　_____

Vocabulary in Context　**6**　To be obscured means to be

☐ a. developed.

☐ b. hidden.

☐ c. viewed.

☐ d. moved.　　　_____

Add your scores for questions 1–6. Enter the total here and on the graph on page 158.　　**Total Score**　_____

16 Habitat

Worms, ants, and flowers live in soil. Fish, crabs, and seaweeds live in oceans. Birds, insects, and moss live in trees. Soil, oceans, and trees are habitats—places where animals and plants live. Besides offering food and shelter, habitats allow for growth and reproduction.

Humans, however, have destroyed many habitats. We change forests into parking lots. We turn grasslands into neighborhoods. We turn beach land into resorts. We turn oceans into chemical dumps. Some plants and animals adapt and survive. Others, however, die. The changes are too much, too fast. Sometimes the death rate becomes greater than the birth rate. Then extinction occurs. An example of this happened on Florida's east coast, the habitat of the dusky seaside sparrow. This habitat changed suddenly as land was developed. And the sparrows were not able to adapt. More sparrows died than were born. In 1987 the dusky seaside sparrow became extinct. None exist in the world today.

Fortunately, <u>conservation</u> efforts are underway. Many states have set aside land for nature preserves. Here, plants and animals live in their natural habitats. Some states have created man-made habitats. Artificial reefs, for example, have been put in ocean waters. The artificial reefs are habitats for hundreds of fish and other marine life. In 1970 the federal government passed a law to protect habitats. This means that the effects of development must be studied. A highway, dam, or power plant may not be built if plants and animals are endangered. We were too late to save the dusky seaside sparrow. Hopefully, however, these new efforts will save other plants and animals.

Main Idea	1	Answer	Score
Mark the *main idea*		M	15
Mark the statement that is *too broad*		B	5
Mark the statement that is *too narrow*		N	5

a. Plant and animal habitats will be destroyed unless we work to protect them. ☐ _____

b. Worms, ants, and flowers live in soil. ☐ _____

c. There are many kinds of habitats. ☐ _____

Subject Matter **2** This passage is concerned with
- ☐ a. federal laws.
- ☐ b. the dusky seaside sparrow.
- ☐ c. habitat protection.
- ☐ d. artificial reefs.

_____

Supporting Details **3** The worst that can happen when habitats are destroyed is that plants and animals
- ☐ a. live in their natural habitats.
- ☐ b. become extinct.
- ☐ c. adapt and survive.
- ☐ d. move to new habitats.

_____

Conclusion **4** The author's feeling about conservation efforts is one of
- ☐ a. surprise.
- ☐ b. disrespect.
- ☐ c. hope.
- ☐ d. enthusiasm.

_____

Clarifying Devices **5** The author explains the effects of habitat destruction by presenting a
- ☐ a. real-life example.
- ☐ b. personal narrative.
- ☐ c. scientific study.
- ☐ d. made-up story.

_____

Vocabulary in Context **6** In this passage, conservation means to
- ☐ a. preserve and protect habitats.
- ☐ b. build highways, dams, and power plants.
- ☐ c. change forests into parking lots.
- ☐ d. guarantee the development of habitats.

_____

Add your scores for questions 1–6. Enter the total here and on the graph on page 158. **Total Score** _____

17 DNA Identification

Have you noticed recent news headlines like these? "Inmates Freed After DNA Tests Prove Innocence." "Thomas Jefferson DNA Study Causes an American Controversy." "DNA Tests Confirm Babies Were Swapped."

Where is your DNA? Sneeze into a tissue—your DNA is on the tissue. Lick an envelope—your DNA is on the seal. In fact, DNA is in every cell of your body.

What is DNA? It is a substance found in the chromosomes of cells. A chromosome is a chain of genes. Each gene carries a piece of information for a trait such as eye color, hair texture, or nose shape. More than one gene is needed for a trait to be expressed. For example, one gene will contain information for skin color. But up to six genes that carry skin color information will produce the color of your skin. Other genes carry a piece of information for other traits. Traits from grandparents, great-grandparents, and so on are passed to you through your parents. All the traits arrange themselves in patterns that are unique. No one, except an identical twin, has the same patterns that you have. DNA acts like a file that stores your unique patterns of traits.

How is DNA used in identification? DNA is obtained from a sample of blood, skin cells, hair, or saliva. The DNA is treated with a chemical, which breaks the DNA into parts. Each part contains one or more patterns of traits. Next, each part of DNA is copied many hundreds of times. Then the parts are put on a gel-like substance, and an electrical current is run through them. The current moves the pieces through the gel, leaving a trail of black bars—like bar codes. Scientists call these bars "DNA fingerprints"; and just like real fingerprints, these DNA prints are distinct for every person (except an identical twin). Scientists use the DNA identification process to <u>confirm</u> the identity of people both living and dead.

Main Idea	1	Answer	Score
	Mark the *main idea*	M	15
	Mark the statement that is *too broad*	B	5
	Mark the statement that is *too narrow*	N	5
	a. DNA is found in cells.	☐	____
	b. No one besides an identical twin has the same DNA as you do.	☐	____
	c. DNA provides information about traits that is being used to identify people.	☐	____

Subject Matter   **2**   This passage is mainly about
- ☐ a. where DNA is found.
- ☐ b. how DNA is used to identify people.
- ☐ c. DNA and identical twins.
- ☐ d. DNA stories in the news.   _____

Supporting Details   **3**   DNA stores each person's
- ☐ a. patterns of traits.
- ☐ b. fingerprints.
- ☐ c. bar codes.
- ☐ d. body cells.   _____

Conclusion   **4**   From information in the passage, which of the following traits can you conclude is **not** a genetic trait?
- ☐ a. having blond hair
- ☐ b. having freckles
- ☐ c. being late often
- ☐ d. having dimples   _____

Clarifying Devices   **5**   The phrase "DNA fingerprint" suggests that DNA
- ☐ a. is shaped like a person's thumb.
- ☐ b. is identified by its swirls.
- ☐ c. has tiny fingers that push it through a cell.
- ☐ d. is as unique as a person's fingerprint.   _____

Vocabulary in Context   **6**   In this passage, <u>confirm</u> means
- ☐ a. strengthen a person's beliefs.
- ☐ b. deny.
- ☐ c. test.
- ☐ d. prove the accuracy of.   _____

Add your scores for questions 1–6. Enter the total here and on the graph on page 158.   **Total Score**   _____

18 Asteroids

Maybe Chicken Little knew about asteroids when she cried, "The sky is falling!" Asteroids are bits of metallic rock that were left over when our solar system was formed. Asteroids vary in size: some are only a few feet wide while others are several hundred miles across. Most asteroids orbit the Sun in a donut-shaped path between Mars and Jupiter. Some asteroids, though, cross the paths of planets. If these asteroids get pushed from their normal orbits, then they may end up in a collision course with a planet. Many asteroids have struck Earth and the moon in the past. Some scientists think that an asteroid six miles wide struck Earth 65 million years ago. The <u>impact</u> might have killed the dinosaurs and other forms of life on Earth.

Astronomers recently discovered asteroid 1997 XF11. The asteroid is one mile wide and traveling at a speed of 45,000 miles per hour. Some astronomers think 1997 XF11 is on a collision course with Earth. Others think the chance of a direct hit is zero. Calculations put the asteroid between 54,000 and 600,000 miles from Earth in the year 2028. If 1997 XF11 hits Earth, it could destroy life on all parts of our planet. Some effects would be tidal waves, fires across whole continents, and a giant dust cloud that would cool the atmosphere and disrupt agriculture.

Astronomers know that Earth will be hit by an asteroid in the future. They have different ideas about how to head off an asteroid impact. One idea is to give each asteroid an "impact risk" number. The higher the number, the greater the chance that the asteroid would hit Earth. If the impact risk is great, then more steps would be taken. Explosives could be put on or near the asteroid. The force of the explosion would push the asteroid away from Earth.

Main Idea	1		Answer	Score
	Mark the *main idea*		M	15
	Mark the statement that is *too broad*		B	5
	Mark the statement that is *too narrow*		N	5
	a. Many objects exist and orbit in space.	☐		_____
	b. Asteroids can cause great damage if they collide with Earth.	☐		_____
	c. Asteroid 1997 XF11 is one mile wide.	☐		_____

Subject Matter   **2**   This passage is mainly about
- ☐ a. asteroids striking Earth.
- ☐ b. 1997 XF11.
- ☐ c. how astronomers discover asteroids.
- ☐ d. how scientists think dinosaurs died.   _____

Supporting Details   **3**   Most asteroids are
- ☐ a. in an orbit around Earth.
- ☐ b. only a few feet wide.
- ☐ c. between Mars and Jupiter.
- ☐ d. on a collision course with Earth.   _____

Conclusion   **4**   An "impact risk" number most resembles a number used
- ☐ a. for a date, like 6/14/01.
- ☐ b. to show time, like 1:15 P.M.
- ☐ c. to show distance, like 4,000 miles.
- ☐ d. to show the strength of an earthquake, like 7.2.   _____

Clarifying Devices   **5**   The author begins the passage with a mention of Chicken Little to
- ☐ a. show that children's stories are usually true.
- ☐ b. get you interested.
- ☐ c. give a clue that the passage will be funny.
- ☐ d. frighten you.   _____

Vocabulary in Context   **6**   In this passage, <u>impact</u> means
- ☐ a. death.
- ☐ b. crash or collision.
- ☐ c. type of metallic rock.
- ☐ d. orbit.   _____

Add your scores for questions 1–6. Enter the total here and on the graph on page 158.   **Total Score**   _____

19 The Scientific Method

Did you ever wonder why the water level in a glass doesn't rise when the ice in the glass melts? To find out why, you can use the scientific method. Used by scientists in various situations, the scientific method is also a clear and logical way to solve many real-world problems, as the procedure below indicates.

Steps in the Scientific Method	Example
State the problem or question.	"Why doesn't the water level in a glass rise when ice melts?"
Using your own observations and research, <u>compile</u> information about the problem.	You already know that ice is frozen water. From your research, you learn that water and ice are made of water molecules.
Form a hypothesis, or a best guess based on the information.	"The molecules in water appear to be closer together than they are in ice."
Test the hypothesis by doing an experiment.	Fill four glasses with ice. Then pour water over the ice and fill each glass to the rim. As the ice melts, you observe that the water level does not go down. Each time you repeat the experiment, you get the same results.
Draw a conclusion based on your results.	Molecules are closer together in water than they are in ice.

Main Idea   1

	Answer	Score
Mark the *main idea*	M	15
Mark the statement that is *too broad*	B	5
Mark the statement that is *too narrow*	N	5

a. Scientists like to figure out problems. ☐ _____

b. One step in the scientific method is to test the hypothesis. ☐ _____

c. The steps in the scientific method help people solve problems. ☐ _____

Score 15 points for each correct answer.   Score

Subject Matter   **2**   Another good title for this passage would be
- [ ] a. Are You Curious?
- [ ] b. Water and Ice Don't Mix.
- [ ] c. Follow the Steps to Find Out Why.
- [ ] d. Hypothesis and Conclusion.

_____

Supporting   **3**   A hypothesis is
Details
- [ ] a. a guess about the cause of something.
- [ ] b. a conclusion about water molecules.
- [ ] c. the first step in the scientific method.
- [ ] d. an experiment.

_____

Conclusion   **4**   This passage suggests that
- [ ] a. doing an experiment will always prove that your hypothesis is correct.
- [ ] b. the scientific method is a logical way to solve problems.
- [ ] c. research should be done only in books.
- [ ] d. few scientists use the scientific method anymore.

_____

Clarifying   **5**   The chart structure in the passage is useful because it
Devices
- [ ] a. compares and contrasts water and ice.
- [ ] b. shows a diagram of how ice melts.
- [ ] c. explains cause and effect.
- [ ] d. clearly shows steps and examples.

_____

Vocabulary   **6**   In this passage, <u>compile</u> means
in Context
- [ ] a. collect.
- [ ] b. lose.
- [ ] c. finish.
- [ ] d. buy.

_____

Add your scores for questions 1–6. Enter the total here   Total
and on the graph on page 158.   Score   _____

20 Sources of Energy

In our lives, we enjoy everything from computers to cars to heated buildings. These comforts have something in common: they all need energy to work. Energy has many different forms. One form, electricity, comes mostly from steam-powered generators. Steam is made by burning coal, oil, or natural gas. Gasoline is another form of energy. Gasoline is made from oil. Oil has many other uses. Paints, fertilizers, and plastics are made from it. We even use it to heat buildings. Coal, oil, and gas are natural resources. We take them from nature to make our lives easier.

We can classify natural resources as either renewable or nonrenewable. Coal, oil, and gas are nonrenewable. They take millions of years to form. Some scientists predict that we will run out of oil and gas in 50 to 100 years. Coal is more plentiful. So it may last for hundreds of years. Resources such as wood and water are renewable. They can be grown or recycled naturally. They can, however, become limited from overuse.

We have developed some alternate sources of energy. But these sources have drawbacks. For example, hydroelectric power, or energy from running water, affects the ecology of surrounding areas. Nuclear power, another alternate source, presents the threat of nuclear accidents. There are also problems related to the storage of nuclear wastes. Solar and wind energies aren't consistent. We can't rely on them. Geothermal energy, caused by heat from inside the earth, is tapped by drawing steam and hot water from pools and geysers. This energy source, like most others, isn't fully developed.

It's time to get serious about energy. We must find practical alternate energy sources. If we wait too long, it will be too late. We will run out of coal, oil, and natural gas. Then we won't have the resources to make alternate energy sources.

Main Idea	1		Answer	Score
		Mark the *main idea*	M	15
		Mark the statement that is *too broad*	B	5
		Mark the statement that is *too narrow*	N	5

a. People enjoy many comforts in their daily lives. ☐ _____

b. Coal, oil, and natural gas are non re-newable resources. ☐ _____

c. People must get serious about developing alternate sources of energy. ☐ _____

Score 15 points for each correct answer.   Score

Subject Matter   **2**   This passage is mainly about
☐ a. putting natural resources into categories.
☐ b. renewable and nonrenewable resources.
☐ c. energy sources and reasons we need new ones.
☐ d. using geothermal energy.   _____

Supporting Details   **3**   Oil and natural gas
☐ a. form in the ground in just a few years.
☐ b. are nonrenewable resources that we may soon use up.
☐ c. may be available for hundreds of years.
☐ d. are found on every continent.   _____

Conclusion   **4**   The second paragraph suggests that renewable resources
☐ a. take millions of years to form.
☐ b. cannot be grown or recycled.
☐ c. will last for hundreds of years.
☐ d. will become scarce if we don't start using them wisely.   _____

Clarifying Devices   **5**   In discussing "alternate forms of energy," the writer
☐ a. tells what is good about them.
☐ b. points out the problems with them.
☐ c. focuses mostly on oil and gas.
☐ d. lists places where they may be found.   _____

Vocabulary in Context   **6**   Drawbacks are
☐ a. pictures.
☐ b. shortcomings.
☐ c. sources of energy.
☐ d. warnings.   _____

Add your scores for questions 1–6. Enter the total here and on the graph on page 158.   Total Score   _____

21 Scientific Classification System

If you collected baseball cards as a child, your collection may have contained hundreds of cards. How did you find one specific card among them all? You might have organized the cards using a method of <u>classification</u>. When you classify things, you group them by their likenesses. For example, baseball cards might be grouped by year, team, or player. You also might use these likenesses to talk to other card collectors. For example, today you might ask a collector, "Do you have a 1999 Chicago Cubs' Sammy Sosa card?" Other collectors know just which card you want by the way you name it.

Living things are classified in a similar way. First, living things are sorted by their likenesses into main groups called *kingdoms*. For example, all animals have these likenesses: they move, and they eat plants or other animals. Because of these similarities, all animals are grouped together. They are in the kingdom Animalia.

Next, the living things in each kingdom are classified into six other groups, each more specific than the last. The chart shows the classification groups for humans.

	Kingdom	Phylum	Class	Order	Family	Genus	Species
Humans	Animalia	Chordata	Mamalia	Primates	Hominidae	*Homo*	*sapiens*

A kingdom is the largest group. A *phylum* is smaller than a kingdom, and a *class* is smaller than a phylum. Since each group is smaller and more specific than the previous one, in a *species,* the smallest group, only things that are very similar are placed. For example, only humans belong to the species *sapiens.* When scientists talk about living things, they name them by their genus and species. Humans belong to genus *Homo* and species *sapiens.* So they are given the scientific name *Homo sapiens.*

Main Idea 1

	Answer	Score
Mark the *main idea*	M	15
Mark the statement that is *too broad*	B	5
Mark the statement that is *too narrow*	N	5

a. The scientific name for humans is *Homo sapiens.* ☐ _____

b. Scientists classify every living thing. ☐ _____

c. A living thing is classified into specific groups by its likenesses. ☐ _____

Subject Matter   2   Another good title for this passage would be
- [ ] a. Sammy Sosa and the Chicago Cubs.
- [ ] b. Humans Are Animals Too.
- [ ] c. Grouping by Likenesses.
- [ ] d. The Five Kingdoms.   _____

Supporting   3   The largest classification group is
Details
- [ ] a. species.
- [ ] b. family.
- [ ] c. class.
- [ ] d. kingdom.   _____

Conclusion   4   The last paragraph suggests that scientists
- [ ] a. use the name *Homo sapiens* when talking about humans.
- [ ] b. communicate frequently about the classification system.
- [ ] c. would be better off naming living things by kingdom and phylum.
- [ ] d. only study large groups of living things.   _____

Clarifying   5   The chart in this passage helps the reader to
Devices
- [ ] a. read details in chronological order.
- [ ] b. see details in their order of importance.
- [ ] c. identify different scientific categories.
- [ ] d. identify cause and effect relationships.   _____

Vocabulary   6   <u>Classification</u> is the process of
in Context
- [ ] a. grouping things according to likenesses.
- [ ] b. arranging plants and animals into one group.
- [ ] c. naming all living things.
- [ ] d. sharing information with other scientists.   _____

Add your scores for questions 1–6. Enter the total here   **Total**
and on the graph on page 158.   **Score**   _____

43

22 Climate

Are you planning a vacation? If you like hot and extremely dry summers, go to Phoenix, Arizona. For hot temperatures but lots of rain and thunderstorms, try Miami, Florida. If you want average temperatures and rainfall, St. Louis, Missouri, is the spot. Or if you're a cold-weather fan, head to Fairbanks, Alaska. Its winters are very cold with very little precipitation. Each of these cities has a certain type of weather. The average weather for a place over many years is called *climate,* and in no two places in the world is it exactly the same. How can this be?

Many things in nature, such as sunshine, temperature, and precipitation, affect climate. Nearness to mountains, oceans, and large lakes affects it too. Another factor is <u>altitude</u>, or height above sea level. Air cools as altitude increases. So a city at a higher altitude may be colder than one at a lower altitude. Finally, winds affect climate. They move heat and moisture between the oceans and continents. Winds keep the tropics from overheating. They keep the polar regions from getting overly cold.

Climate changes over long periods of time. Some scientists think, for example, that the earth's climate changed at the time of the dinosaurs. They think the dinosaurs died because of the change. What causes a climate to change? One possible cause may be changes in the sun. Sunspots, for example, are cool, dark spots that form on the sun. Sunspots may decrease precipitation on the earth and cause unusually dry periods. Changes in the atmosphere may change climate too. Volcanic eruptions, for instance, release solid particles into the air. These particles may form a cloud that blocks out the sun's heat. Human activity is another cause of climate change. Air pollution and the reduction of forest cover may have long-term effects on climate.

Main Idea	1	Answer	Score
	Mark the *main idea*	M	15
	Mark the statement that is *too broad*	B	5
	Mark the statement that is *too narrow*	N	5

		Answer	Score
a.	Climate varies from place to place.	☐	____
b.	The climate of Phoenix is hot and extremely dry.	☐	____
c.	Climate is a long-term pattern of weather, but some things can change it.	☐	____

Score 15 points for each correct answer.   **Score**

Subject Matter   2   This passage is concerned with things that affect
☐ a. precipitation.
☐ b. climate.
☐ c. altitude.
☐ d. sunspots.

_____

Supporting Details   3   Change in climate may have caused
☐ a. dinosaurs to die.
☐ b. dark spots to form on the sun.
☐ c. volcanic eruptions.
☐ d. air pollution.

_____

Conclusion   4   The effect of a volcanic eruption on climate may be to make it
☐ a. wetter.
☐ b. dryer.
☐ c. warmer.
☐ d. colder.

_____

Clarifying Devices   5   To help readers understand how climate can change, the writer uses
☐ a. examples.
☐ b. a story about the seashore.
☐ c. order of importance.
☐ d. a strong argument.

_____

Vocabulary in Context   6   Which of the following is the place of greatest altitude on a mountain?
☐ a. the foot of the mountain
☐ b. the side of the mountain
☐ c. the top of the mountain
☐ d. the ridge of the mountain

_____

Add your scores for questions 1–6. Enter the total here and on the graph on page 158.   **Total Score**

_____

23 Cell Structure

You are an <u>organism</u>. Some organisms consist of only a single living cell, but humans are made of trillions of living cells. Like you, many plants and animals are also made of numerous living cells. The diagram below shows the main parts of an animal cell—see if you can identify them as you read.

A cell is covered by a thin layer called a *cell membrane*. The cell membrane has pores, or small openings, in it that allow food and other substances to enter and leave the cell. A jellylike substance called *cytoplasm* fills the inside of a cell. The parts of the cell float in the cytoplasm.

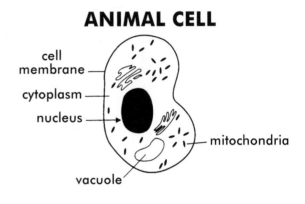

ANIMAL CELL

Each part of the cell performs a specific function. Near the center of the cell is the *nucleus,* the "control center" of the cell. It contains information that directs all cellular activities. *Chromosomes* inside the nucleus carry the directions for making new cells. The nucleus is covered by the *nuclear membrane.* It contains pores to let food and other substances in and out of the nucleus. The sausage-shaped *mitochondria* change food materials into energy for the cell. *Vacuoles* store food and water.

Main Idea	1		Answer	Score
	Mark the *main idea*		M	15
	Mark the statement that is *too broad*		B	5
	Mark the statement that is *too narrow*		N	5

    a. The various parts of a cell all have their own jobs to do. ☐ _____

    b. The nucleus controls activities in the other parts of the cell. ☐ _____

    c. Humans are made of trillions of cells. ☐ _____

Score 15 points for each correct answer. Score

Subject Matter   **2**   Another good title for this passage would be
☐ a. How to Change Food into Energy.
☐ b. The Mystery of Pores.
☐ c. The Transportation System of a Cell.
☐ d. How a Cell Works. _____

Supporting   **3**   The special job of vacuoles is to
Details   ☐ a. let food in and out of the nucleus.
☐ b. make new cells.
☐ c. allow substances into and out of the cell.
☐ d. store food and water. _____

Conclusion   **4**   The arrow on the cell diagram points to
☐ a. the cell membrane.
☐ b. the nucleus.
☐ c. one of the mitochondria.
☐ d. one of the vacuoles. _____

Clarifying   **5**   The term "control center" in the final paragraph
Devices   suggests that the nucleus functions like
☐ a. an airport tower.
☐ b. a traffic jam.
☐ c. a bus.
☐ d. any vehicle with wheels. _____

Vocabulary   **6**   An <u>organism</u> is a
in Context   ☐ a. musical instrument.
☐ b. mixture of dead plants and animals.
☐ c. nonliving substance.
☐ d. living thing. _____

Add your scores for questions 1–6. Enter the total here   **Total**
and on the graph on page 158.   **Score** _____

24 The Human Body

Human beings are recognized by such <u>external</u> body parts as the head, torso, arms, legs, and skin. On the inside, however, human beings are marvelously complex. Inside the human body are 206 bones and about 700 muscles; a brain of about 10 billion nerve cells; a small intestine about 22 feet long; a heart that beats more than 3 billion times during a lifetime; and a network of blood vessels that, if laid end to end, would encircle the earth's equator more than twice. These are just a few internal parts of the human body. What's amazing is that all parts of the human body work together. To understand how, let's start with the basics.

The human body contains about 100 trillion different *cells*. Some are bone and blood cells. Others include muscle, epithelial, and nerve cells. When similar cells group together to perform the same task, they are called *tissue*. Epithelial cells, for example, group together to form epithelial tissue. This tissue lines and protects your nose, throat, windpipe, and digestive tract. You also know this tissue as skin, which protects your body. Other tissues include blood tissue, muscle tissue, and nerve tissue.

Different tissues that work together to do a particular job are called an *organ*. Epithelial tissue, muscle tissue, blood tissue, and nerve tissue, for instance, form an organ called the *lungs*. The lungs add oxygen and remove carbon dioxide from the blood when we breathe. Other organs include the heart, stomach, liver, and intestines. Organs, tissues, and other body structures work together to form body systems. Each body system performs a special job. The nose, throat, and lungs, for example, form the respiratory system. This system controls our breathing. Other body systems include the circulatory system, digestive system, and skeletal system. When all body systems work together, the human body has life.

Main Idea	1		
		Answer	**Score**
Mark the *main idea*		M	15
Mark the statement that is *too broad*		B	5
Mark the statement that is *too narrow*		N	5
a. Humans are very complex.		☐	_____
b. The human body contains 206 bones and about 700 muscles.		☐	_____
c. The various elements of the body work together to give it life.		☐	_____

Subject Matter　**2**　The purpose of this passage is to
- [ ] a. compare the digestive and skeletal systems.
- [ ] b. describe the purpose of the small intestine.
- [ ] c. explain how the parts of the human body work together.
- [ ] d. list every part of the human body.　　　____

Supporting Details　**3**　Epithelial tissue is epithelial cells that group together to
- [ ] a. line and protect your nose and throat.
- [ ] b. give the body support and movement.
- [ ] c. control breathing.
- [ ] d. remove carbon dioxide from the blood.　　____

Conclusion　**4**　After reading this passage, we can conclude that the writer has
- [ ] a. mentioned every part of the body.
- [ ] b. shown how organs are the same as tissues.
- [ ] c. mentioned some major body elements.
- [ ] d. described body elements in spatial order.　　____

Clarifying Devices　**5**　The order in which information in the passage is presented is
- [ ] a. cells, tissue, organs, body systems.
- [ ] b. cells, organs, body systems, tissue.
- [ ] c. body systems, cells, tissue, organs.
- [ ] d. cells, organs, tissue, body systems.　　____

Vocabulary in Context　**6**　In this passage, the word <u>external</u> means
- [ ] a. situated on the inside of the body.
- [ ] b. seen on the outside of the body.
- [ ] c. something that is not significant.
- [ ] d. an outside force.　　____

Add your scores for questions 1–6. Enter the total here and on the graph on page 158.　　Total Score　____

25 Animal Behavior

Ants release scent spots to guide them through mazes. Honeybees recognize land-marks to find their way home. Groundhogs hibernate to survive cold winters. All of these are examples of animal behavior.

Behavior is the response of an organism to the things around it. Some behavior is a response to an external, or outside, stimulus in the environment. A mouse, for example, runs when it sees a cat. The running is the response to the external stimulus of the cat. Other behavior is a response to an <u>internal</u> stimulus. An example is a hungry cat chasing a mouse. The chasing is the response to the internal stimulus of hunger.

There are two types of behavior: innate and learned. *Innate behavior* is an automatic inherited response. Reflexes and instincts are both innate behaviors. A *reflex* is a direct immediate response to a stimulus. A reflex, for example, enables a cat to land on its feet most of the time. An *instinct* is a series of actions in response to a stimulus. An instinct, for instance, enables a newborn mammal to find and feed from its mother's breast. Other instincts are animal migration, mating, and hibernation.

Learned behavior is behavior that changes due to experience. One way it may be learned is through trial and error. A bird building its first nest, for example, collects a variety of materials including twigs, plastic, and paper. The bird soon learns that only twigs make a sturdy nest. Eventually, the bird modifies its behavior and collects only twigs. Behavior also may be learned from association with a stimulus. An example is people standing at a pond throwing bread crumbs into it. Fish in the pond see the people and then the food. The fish come to the surface and eat. The fish eventually associate the stimulus of people with food. The fish respond by coming to the surface whenever people are there, even if they don't toss bread crumbs.

Main Idea	1	Answer	Score
	Mark the *main idea*	M	15
	Mark the statement that is *too broad*	B	5
	Mark the statement that is *too narrow*	N	5
	a. All animals have behaviors.	☐	_____
	b. Behavior is the response of an organism to the things around it.	☐	_____
	c. Some behaviors are learned by trial and error.	☐	_____

Score 15 points for each correct answer. Score

Subject Matter 2 The purpose of this passage is to
☐ a. explain types of animal behavior.
☐ b. explain what an instinct is.
☐ c. describe animal hibernation.
☐ d. give an example of trial and error learning. _____

Supporting Details 3 Animal migration is an example of
☐ a. an instinct.
☐ b. trial and error.
☐ c. an external stimulus.
☐ d. a learned behavior. _____

Conclusion 4 An external stimulus might cause you as a human to
☐ a. eat when you are hungry.
☐ b. laugh when you hear a funny joke.
☐ c. sleep when you are tired.
☐ d. drink water when you are thirsty. _____

Clarifying Devices 5 To help the reader understand the terms in this passage, the author presents
☐ a. arguments and opinions.
☐ b. definitions and examples.
☐ c. comparisons and contrasts.
☐ d. scientific experiments and studies. _____

Vocabulary in Context 6 In this passage, the word <u>internal</u> means
☐ a. above.
☐ b. below.
☐ c. outside.
☐ d. inside. _____

Add your scores for questions 1–6. Enter the total here and on the graph on page 158. Total Score _____

26 Life Science and Physical Science

There are many branches of science that you may study. Basically, though, all of these fall into two major areas—life science and physical science.

Life science is the study of life and living things. This is the organic world. This is where each living thing carries out life processes. (Life processes are things like growing and reproducing.) Physical science is the study of the <u>inorganic</u> world. It studies nonliving things. Nonliving things do not carry out life processes.

Life science is also called biology. Two areas of biology are zoology and botany. Zoology is the study of animals. Botany is the study of plants. Some biologists study how organisms carry out life processes. This is physiology. Other scientists study how parents and offspring are alike and different. This is genetics. Some biologists specialize in a combination of subjects. An example is paleontology. It is the study of ancient life. It combines the studies of earth science, zoology, and botany.

The area of physical science includes four big subjects. One is physics. It is the study of energy. It includes the structure and behavior of atoms. Another is chemistry. It is the study of matter. It studies matter's properties and structure and the ways it changes. A third is astronomy. This is the science of the entire universe beyond Earth. It also studies Earth when Earth interacts with other bodies in the solar system. A fourth is earth science. This is the study of Earth and the space surrounding it. Different branches of earth science study land, water, and air. These are the sciences of geology, oceanography, and meteorology.

Main Idea	1		
		Answer	**Score**
Mark the *main idea*		M	15
Mark the statement that is *too broad*		B	5
Mark the statement that is *too narrow*		N	5
a. Our universe is studied scientifically.		☐	_____
b. Life science is the study of life and living things.		☐	_____
c. Science involves two major areas, life science and physical science.		☐	_____

Subject Matter   **2**   The purpose of this passage is mainly to
☐ a. give a history of science study.
☐ b. define life science and physical science.
☐ c. explore careers in science.
☐ d. predict future trends in science.   _____

Supporting Details   **3**   Chemistry
☐ a. is one of the life sciences.
☐ b. is the study of matter and its properties.
☐ c. looks at life processes.
☐ d. studies the organic world.   _____

Conclusion   **4**   An area that would be studied in life science would be
☐ a. human diseases.
☐ b. sunspots.
☐ c. snow.
☐ d. volcanoes.   _____

Clarifying Devices   **5**   The writer helps to make clear the four categories of physical science by
☐ a. using signal and transitional words.
☐ b. using similes and metaphors.
☐ c. presenting them in order of importance.
☐ d. presenting them in chronological order.   _____

Vocabulary in Context   **6**   The word <u>inorganic</u> means
☐ a. physical.
☐ b. scientific.
☐ c. nonliving.
☐ d. living.   _____

Add your scores for questions 1–6. Enter the total here and on the graph on page 159.   **Total Score**   _____

27 Plate Tectonics: A Very Slow Ride

The surface of the earth may seem very <u>stable</u> to you. But you might be amazed if you knew some of the things that were going on under that surface.

The earth has an outer shell of rigid pieces called *tectonic plates*. The plates include both ocean floor and dry land. Some have whole continents on top of them. These plates are estimated to be about six to ten miles thick under the oceans and as much as 120 miles thick under some continents. The continents on top of the plates are just going along for a slow ride, moving only about four inches per year. But even this small movement causes three types of big interactions.

One type is ocean ridges. These ridges develop in places where two plates are moving away from each other. As the plates separate, hot magma flows up to fill the space. New crust builds up on the plate boundaries and causes ocean ridges. These ridges form long mountain ranges, which only rise above the ocean surface in a few places.

Another type of reaction—trenches—occurs between two plates that are moving toward each other. As the plates meet, one bends downward and plunges underneath the other. This forms deep ocean trenches. The Marianas Trench off Guam in the western Pacific Ocean has a depth of more than 36,000 feet. This is the lowest point on the ocean floor. If the leading edges of the two colliding plates carry continents, then the layers of rock in the overriding plate crumple and fold. A plate that carried what is now India collided with the southern edge of the plate that carried Europe and most of Asia. This caused the Himalayas, the world's highest mountains.

The third reaction is transform faults. These faults occur where two plates that are traveling in opposite directions slide past each other. Severe earthquakes can occur. The San Andreas Fault in California is a good example of this type of movement.

Main Idea	1	Answer	Score
	Mark the *main idea*	M	15
	Mark the statement that is *too broad*	B	5
	Mark the statement that is *too narrow*	N	5

a. Tectonic plates cause three types of movements of the earth's surface. ☐ _____

b. The movement of tectonic plates may cause earthquakes. ☐ _____

c. The earth has a shell of tectonic plates. ☐ _____

Score 15 points for each correct answer. Score

Subject Matter **2** This passage is mostly about
☐ a. effects of movements of the earth's plates.
☐ b. types of continents.
☐ c. the Marianas Trench.
☐ d. transform faults. _____

Supporting Details **3** The San Andreas Fault is an example of
☐ a. a California rock formation.
☐ b. a severe earthquake.
☐ c. a trench.
☐ d. two plates traveling in opposite directions. _____

Conclusion **4** According to information in this passage, the earth
☐ a. is always changing.
☐ b. never changes.
☐ c. is shrinking.
☐ d. is melting. _____

Clarifying Devices **5** To explain an effect of trenches, the writer gives the example of
☐ a. the sea floor near Guam.
☐ b. India.
☐ c. the San Andreas Fault.
☐ d. the Himalayan Mountains. _____

Vocabulary in Context **6** In this passage, the word stable means
☐ a. a place for horses.
☐ b. calm and easygoing.
☐ c. steady or firm.
☐ d. a collection of animals. _____

Add your scores for questions 1–6. Enter the total here and on the graph on page 159. Total Score _____

28 An Essential Scientific Process

All life on the earth depends upon green plants. Using sunlight, the plants produce their own food. Then animals feed upon the plants. They take in the nutrients the plants have made and stored. But that's not all. Sunlight also helps a plant produce oxygen. Some of the oxygen is used by the plant, but a plant usually produces more oxygen than it uses. The <u>excess</u> oxygen is needed by animals and other organisms.

The process of changing light into food and oxygen is called *photosynthesis*. Besides light energy from the sun, plants also use water and carbon dioxide. The water gets to the plant through its roots. The carbon dioxide enters the leaves through tiny openings called *stomata*. The carbon dioxide travels to chloroplasts, special cells in the bodies of green plants. This is where photosynthesis takes place. Chloroplasts contain the chlorophylls that give plants their green color. The chlorophylls are the molecules that trap light energy. The trapped light energy changes water and carbon dioxide to produce oxygen and a simple sugar called *glucose*.

Carbon dioxide and oxygen move into and out of the stomata. Water vapor also moves out of the stomata. More than 90 percent of the water a plant takes in through its roots escapes through the stomata. During the daytime, the stomata of most plants are open. This allows carbon dioxide to enter the leaves for photosynthesis. As night falls, carbon dioxide is not needed. The stomata of most plants close. Water loss stops.

If photosynthesis ceased, there would be little food or other organic matter on the earth. Most organisms would disappear. The earth's atmosphere would no longer contain oxygen. Photosynthesis is essential for life on our planet.

Main Idea 1		Answer	Score
Mark the *main idea*		M	15
Mark the statement that is *too broad*		B	5
Mark the statement that is *too narrow*		N	5
a. Stomata allow carbon dioxide to enter leaves for photosynthesis.		☐	_____
b. Life on the earth depends upon green plants.		☐	_____
c. The process of changing light into food and oxygen is called photosynthesis.		☐	_____

Subject Matter   **2**   Another good title for this passage would be
☐ a. Oxygen and Carbon Dioxide.
☐ b. Plants and Their Roots.
☐ c. How Photosynthesis Works.
☐ d. Why Our Earth Needs Water.

_____

Supporting Details   **3**   Which of the following does *not* move through a plant's stomata?
☐ a. carbon dioxide
☐ b. water vapor
☐ c. oxygen
☐ d. food

_____

Conclusion   **4**   In the title, the term *Essential Scientific Process* refers to
☐ a. photosynthesis.
☐ b. the formation of glucose.
☐ c. global warming.
☐ d. water getting to the roots of plants.

_____

Clarifying Devices   **5**   This passage is primarily developed by
☐ a. explaining a process.
☐ b. telling a story.
☐ c. comparing and contrasting.
☐ d. convincing the reader of plants' importance.

_____

Vocabulary in Context   **6**   In this passage, excess means
☐ a. heavy.
☐ b. extra.
☐ c. green.
☐ d. liquid.

_____

Add your scores for questions 1–6. Enter the total here and on the graph on page 159.   **Total Score**

_____

29 Black Holes

Most scientists agree that black holes exist but are nearly impossible to locate. A black hole in the universe is not a solid object, like a planet, but it is shaped like a sphere. Astronomers think that at the center of a black hole there is a single point in space with infinite density (in other words, there are no limits to its denseness). This single point is called a *singularity*. The singularity theory says that when a massive star collapses, all the material in it disappears into the singularity. The center of a black hole would not really be a hole at all but an infinitely dense point.

A black hole also has no surface. It begins at a gravitational place whose outer limits are called the event horizon. The event horizon is the point of no return. Anything that crosses the event horizon is pulled in by the black hole's great gravity.

Although black holes do exist, they are difficult to observe. These are the reasons.

- No light or anything else comes out of black holes. As a result, they are invisible to a telescope.
- In astronomical terms, black holes are truly tiny. For example, a black hole formed by the collapse of a giant star would have an event horizon only 18 miles across.
- The nearest black holes would be dozens of light years away from Earth. One light year is the distance light travels in a year. It is about 6 trillion miles. Even the most powerful telescopes could not pick out an object so small at such a great distance.

In 1994 the Hubble Space Telescope provided evidence that black holes exist. There are still answers to be found, however, so black holes remain one of the mysteries of the universe.

Main Idea	1	Answer	Score
	Mark the *main idea*	M	15
	Mark the statement that is *too broad*	B	5
	Mark the statement that is *too narrow*	N	5
	a. Black holes are part of space.	☐	_____
	b. Black holes exist but are difficult to observe.	☐	_____
	c. Black holes are infinitely dense.	☐	_____

Subject Matter   **2**   Another good title for this passage would be

☐ a. Black Holes Allow Nothing to Escape!

☐ b. Black Holes: A Mystery to Be Solved.

☐ c. The Universe Holds Many Secrets.

☐ d. Traveling to a Black Hole.   _____

Supporting Details   **3**   The center of a black hole is

☐ a. infinite in size.

☐ b. not really a hole at all.

☐ c. empty.

☐ d. a huge, massive star.   _____

Conclusion   **4**   A black hole is like a planet in that both

☐ a. support life.

☐ b. are spherical in shape.

☐ c. are solid.

☐ d. are invisible to telescopes.   _____

Clarifying Devices   **5**   The three bulleted points support the statement that

☐ a. black holes are difficult to find.

☐ b. no light can escape from black holes.

☐ c. black holes do exist.

☐ d. black holes do not exist.   _____

Vocabulary in Context   **6**   The word <u>massive</u> means very

☐ a. bright.

☐ b. fast.

☐ c. far away.

☐ d. large.   _____

Add your scores for questions 1–6. Enter the total here and on the graph on page 159.   **Total Score**   _____

30 Unlocking the Human Genome

A project to unlock secrets—what scientist could resist that challenge? This is what many scientists are doing as they work on the Human Genome Project. The aim of the project is to decode all of the some 100,000 genes in the human body. Scientists are using DNA fingerprinting techniques to do the decoding.

DNA is the substance found in the chromosomes of a cell. A chromosome is a chain of genes. Each gene carries a piece of information. At any one moment in a cell, thousands of genes are turned on and off to produce proteins. The challenge for scientists is to find out what role each gene plays in protein production. At some point, this decoding will be complete. Then scientists will have a map of an ideal genome, or a picture of the total genetic nature of a human being. The ideal genome is called a consensus genome. Everything works well in a consensus genome.

But no one in the world has a consensus genome. Everyone's genome is different from the ideal. These differences are referred to as genetic <u>mutations</u>. Genetic mutations in a person's genome mean that the person has a greater than average chance of suffering from health problems. Problems such as baldness, stuttering, and mild headaches are not life-threatening. But problems such as schizophrenia, heart disease, and diabetes are serious.

It will take years to identify the role of each of the 100,000 genes. The short-term goal of the project is to find the physical and mental health problems a person is likely to encounter during his or her lifetime. The long-term goal is to have each person live a longer, healthier life.

Main Idea	1		Answer	Score
	Mark the *main idea*		M	15
	Mark the statement that is *too broad*		B	5
	Mark the statement that is *too narrow*		N	5

a. The human body has about 100,000 genes. ☐ _____

b. The Human Genome Project is trying to decode the genes in the human body. ☐ _____

c. Scientists unlock secrets. ☐ _____

Subject Matter 2 This passage is mostly about
    ☐ a. how DNA works.
    ☐ b. decoding all the genes in the human body.
    ☐ c. illnesses like diabetes.
    ☐ d. the future of science.   _____

Supporting Details 3 A chromosome is a
    ☐ a. fingerprint.
    ☐ b. substance called DNA.
    ☐ c. colorful cell.
    ☐ d. chain of genes.   _____

Conclusion 4 The Human Genome Project is mainly a scientific
    ☐ a. challenge.
    ☐ b. agreement.
    ☐ c. debate.
    ☐ d. law.   _____

Clarifying Devices 5 The first sentence in this passage is intended to
    ☐ a. make you angry.
    ☐ b. arouse your interest.
    ☐ c. confuse you.
    ☐ d. present the main idea.   _____

Vocabulary in Context 6 Mutations are
    ☐ a. experiments.
    ☐ b. disagreements.
    ☐ c. differences or changes.
    ☐ d. people who do not live on Earth.   _____

Add your scores for questions 1–6. Enter the total here   Total
and on the graph on page 159.   Score   _____

31 Sunspots

It's not surprising that sunspots were observed by ancient astronomers. The largest sunspots on the sun can be seen without a telescope. It was not until the invention of the telescope in the early 17th century, however, that systematic studies of sunspots could be undertaken. The great astronomer Galileo was among the first to make telescopic observations of sunspots.

Sunspots are regions of extremely strong magnetic fields found on the sun's surface. A sunspot has a dark central core known as the *umbra*. The umbra is surrounded by a dark ring called the *penumbra,* where the magnetic field spreads outward. Sunspots appear dark because they are giving off less radiation than the areas around them. Sunspots are cooler than the rest of the sun's surface.

Sunspots are frequently observed in pairs or in paired groups. The members of a spot pair are identified as the leading spot and the following spot. They are identified by their position in the pair in terms of the direction in which the sun rotates.

The number of sunspots at any one time varies. Sometimes there may be as many as 10 groups and 300 spots across the sun. A large spot group may consist of as many as 200 spots. The number of spots changes in a fairly regular pattern called the *sunspot cycle*. The largest number occurs about every 11 years. At sunspot minimum, there are at most just a few small spots.

The average lifetime of an individual spot group is roughly one solar rotation, which is about 25 days. The most <u>persistent</u> large spots, however, can survive for two to three months.

Main Idea	1	Answer	Score
	Mark the *main idea*	M	15
	Mark the statement that is *too broad*	B	5
	Mark the statement that is *too narrow*	N	5

a. Sunspots appear on the sun. ☐ _____

b. Sunspots, regions of magnetic fields on the sun's surface, occur at fairly regular intervals. ☐ _____

c. Large sunspots can be seen without a telescope. ☐ _____

Subject Matter   **2**   This passage is mainly
- ☐ a. a description of sunspots.
- ☐ b. a discussion of why sunspots occur.
- ☐ c. an explanation of the sun's movements.
- ☐ d. a biography of Galileo.   _____

Supporting Details   **3**   Leading spot and following spot are
- ☐ a. the names of spots in a spot pair.
- ☐ b. the direction of the sun's rotation.
- ☐ c. names of the two largest sunspots.
- ☐ d. names of a sunspot's central core and the ring around the core.   _____

Conclusion   **4**   If there had been heavy sunspot activity in 1857, the next heavy outbreak would have been in
- ☐ a. 1858.
- ☐ b. 1862.
- ☐ c. 1865.
- ☐ d. 1868.   _____

Clarifying Devices   **5**   The first paragraph presents sunspots through
- ☐ a. an explanation of how they work.
- ☐ b. a descriptive perspective.
- ☐ c. a historical perspective.
- ☐ d. a cause and effect perspective.   _____

Vocabulary in Context   **6**   In this passage, persistent means
- ☐ a. quickly disappearing.
- ☐ b. large.
- ☐ c. lasting.
- ☐ d. having a dark, reddish brown color.   _____

Add your scores for questions 1–6. Enter the total here and on the graph on page 159.   **Total Score**   _____

32 Recognizing Volcanoes

Volcanoes may assume a variety of shapes. These are determined by the composition of the magma, or hot melted rock, that lies within them. The shapes are also determined by their past eruptions. The four main volcano forms are identified by the shape of their cones. These include cinder cones, shield volcanoes, composite cones, and domes.

Cinder cones are the simplest type of volcano. They form when an eruption throws out rocks and ash but little flowing lava. Cinder cones usually consist of small volcanic fragments that are as fine as ash or as large as a pebble. The cinder cone of Paricutín in Mexico began in a flat cornfield in 1943. It reached a height of 1,300 feet before becoming <u>dormant</u>.

Nonexplosive eruptions with easy flowing lava produce *shield volcanoes*. The flow pours out in all directions, building a broad, gently sloping cone. The lava flows from shield volcanoes are usually only 3 to 33 feet thick, but they may spread out for long distances. The name *shield* comes from their resemblance to the shields of early Germanic warriors. The volcanoes of Hawaii and Iceland are shield volcanoes.

Alternating eruptions of ash and rocks followed by quiet lava flows form strong, steep-sided volcanic cones called *composite cones*. Most of the tallest volcanoes on the continents are composite volcanoes. Mount St. Helens in Washington is an example of such a volcano.

Domes are built by a lava so thick that it barely flows. When a dome plugs the vent of a volcano, pressure builds up under the dome. This may result in a future eruption. Domes often form in the craters of composite volcanoes, such as the one that has recently developed in the crater of Mount St. Helens.

Main Idea	1		Answer	Score
	Mark the *main idea*		M	15
	Mark the statement that is *too broad*		B	5
	Mark the statement that is *too narrow*		N	5

    a. The tallest volcanoes on the continents are composite volcanoes. ☐ _____

    b. Volcanic forms are identified by the shape of their cones. ☐ _____

    c. Volcanoes have a variety of shapes. ☐ _____

Subject Matter   **2**   Which fictional Internet Web site would most likely produce the information found in this passage?

☐ a. volcano_dwellers@botany.gov

☐ b. reachingskyward@astronomy.net

☐ c. rocks-lava-ashes@geology.com

☐ d. old.old.stuff@paleontology.edu   _____

Supporting Details   **3**   Paricutín is an example of a

☐ a. shield volcano.

☐ b. dome.

☐ c. cinder cone.

☐ d. composite cone.   _____

Conclusion   **4**   This passage leads the reader to conclude that

☐ a. all volcanoes have cinder cones.

☐ b. volcanoes can be grouped by their similarities.

☐ c. like snowflakes, no two volcanoes are alike.

☐ d. all volcanoes explode regularly.   _____

Clarifying Devices   **5**   The words in _italic_ type are

☐ a. supporting details.

☐ b. names of important places.

☐ c. key words.

☐ d. definitions.   _____

Vocabulary in Context   **6**   In this passage, <u>dormant</u> means

☐ a. inactive.

☐ b. tired.

☐ c. lively.

☐ d. noticeable.   _____

Add your scores for questions 1–6. Enter the total here and on the graph on page 159.   **Total Score**   _____

33 Making Silicon Chips

It was originally called the *monolithic integrated circuit.* Since its development in 1958, it has gotten smaller and more complex, but its name has become less complicated. Today it is called the *silicon chip,* and it is contained in many things that you use every day. You'll find it in your pocket calculator, computer, microwave oven, and cellular phone.

This powerful <u>miniaturized</u> electrical circuit begins with quartz crystal, or silica. Quartz is the main ingredient in a silicon chip. Found in many stones and sand, it is the earth's second most abundant element. The quartz crystal is mined and sent to the chip factory. There it is converted into a 264-pound rod of pure silicon. The rod is sliced into very thin wafers. Each wafer is washed, polished, cleaned, and carefully inspected. Then the wafers are coated with a layer of electrical insulation.

Meanwhile, designers have used a computer to map out the electrical circuit they need. They make a mask, or pattern, of the circuit. Then they reduce the mask and duplicate it hundreds of times. The masks are used to stencil many circuit patterns at one time onto the wafer. This process is performed several times, overlaying layers of the circuit. A complicated chip might have as many as 20 overlaid masks.

The finished individual chips are cut from the wafer, and connecting wires are bonded onto each chip. Because the chip is usually less than the size of a fingernail, each one is placed into a frame. The frame is sealed in a plastic case, and legs are bent down ready to be inserted into a circuit board. The process—from wafer to chip—includes several hundred steps and takes about 45 days.

Main Idea	1	Answer	Score
	Mark the *main idea*	M	15
	Mark the statement that is *too broad*	B	5
	Mark the statement that is *too narrow*	N	5
	a. Silicon chips are very useful.	☐	____
	b. Quartz is the main ingredient in a silicon chip.	☐	____
	c. Silicon chips are produced in a lengthy, complicated process.	☐	____

Subject Matter   **2**   This passage is primarily about
- ☐ a. mining.
- ☐ b. computers.
- ☐ c. the making of miniature electrical circuits.
- ☐ d. products that are used every day.   _____

Supporting Details   **3**   Wafers are washed and polished
- ☐ a. after the wafers are cut from the rod.
- ☐ b. before the wafers are cut from the rod.
- ☐ c. after the mask is laid on the wafers.
- ☐ d. when the quartz crystal is mined.   _____

Conclusion   **4**   The final sentence is a reference to the
- ☐ a. simplicity of making a silicon chip.
- ☐ b. size of a silicon chip.
- ☐ c. complexity of making a silicon chip.
- ☐ d. quality of a silicon chip.   _____

Clarifying Devices   **5**   The structure of this passage is
- ☐ a. steps in a process.
- ☐ b. cause and effect.
- ☐ c. question and answer.
- ☐ d. compare and contrast.   _____

Vocabulary in Context   **6**   The word <u>miniaturized</u> in this passage means
- ☐ a. involving tiny toys.
- ☐ b. involving a difficult process.
- ☐ c. made larger.
- ☐ d. made smaller.   _____

Add your scores for questions 1–6. Enter the total here and on the graph on page 159.   **Total Score**   _____

34 A Little Lamp to Read By

Thomas A. Edison said he would invent an inexpensive incandescent bulb that would burn for hundreds of hours. He was sure that people really wanted a soft, mellow little lamp to read by. The problem was the filament. This was the thin wire inside the vacuum-sealed globe that would provide the light. He couldn't find a material with such a high resistance and melting point that only a small amount of electric current would make it glow for thousands of hours.

Then, on October 21, 1879, a horseshoe-shaped filament of sewing thread in a vacuum-sealed glass globe burned for $14\frac{1}{2}$ hours. Edison knew he was on the right track. The thread had been coated with powdered carbon and cooked in a furnace. It had been carbonized. In the months to come, Edison and his assistants would have everything in sight carbonized—wood shavings, fishing line, cork, even a hair from an assistant's beard—in their search for the right material.

After months of methodical testing, the answer came quite by accident. As Edison idly ran his fingers along a palm-leaf fan, the texture of the hard bamboo rim caught his attention. Well, why not? They'd tried everything else. The bamboo fibers, carbonized and carefully assembled into a paper-thin filament, proved sturdier and longer-lasting than anything else.

Immediately the Great Bamboo Hunt began. Edison sent out <u>scouts</u> to bring back samples of every variety on earth. They brought back more than 6,000 bamboo samples. All were carbonized and tested, but the best came from a plantation in Japan. In the years to come, this plantation would supply the filament material for millions of lamps around the world.

Main Idea 1		Answer	Score
Mark the *main idea*		M	15
Mark the statement that is *too broad*		B	5
Mark the statement that is *too narrow*		N	5

a. Thomas A. Edison was a famous inventor. ☐ _____

b. The best filament material came from Japan. ☐ _____

c. Incandescent bulbs were not useful until the right filament was found. ☐ _____

Subject Matter   **2**   Another good title for this passage would be
- ☐ a. The Search for the Right Filament.
- ☐ b. Edison, the Great Inventor.
- ☐ c. Hunting for Bamboo.
- ☐ d. Working with a Vacuum Tube.   _____

Supporting Details   **3**   Edison looked for
- ☐ a. a filament material with high resistance and a high melting point.
- ☐ b. a vacuum-sealed glass globe.
- ☐ c. an electric current.
- ☐ d. a palm-leaf fan with a hard bamboo rim.   _____

Conclusion   **4**   Edison's discovery was the result of his personal
- ☐ a. appearance.
- ☐ b. friends.
- ☐ c. persistence.
- ☐ d. property.   _____

Clarifying Devices   **5**   Wood shavings, fishing line, cork, and hair are examples of
- ☐ a. the right filament materials.
- ☐ b. materials that Edison tested.
- ☐ c. things that will burn in a furnace.
- ☐ d. things that can be made into thread.   _____

Vocabulary in Context   **6**   In this passage, scouts means
- ☐ a. people sent to get information.
- ☐ b. young members of a pack or troop.
- ☐ c. Native American guides.
- ☐ d. rude, unpleasant people.   _____

Add your scores for questions 1–6. Enter the total here and on the graph on page 159.   **Total Score**   _____

35 The Good Mother Dinosaur

Jack Horner was on a fossil-hunting trip in Montana in 1978 when a stony bump in a pasture caught his attention. Pebbles and gray-black stone were scattered over it. Horner and fellow fossil-hunter Bob Makela had found the bones of two baby duckbilled dinosaurs. These were the bones of hadrosaurs, some of the most commonly found dinosaur fossils in the American West. So Horner and Makela had not found anything unusual yet. When they dug further, however, they realized that they had found the first dinosaur nest ever discovered in North America.

Over the next six summers, Horner and his crew returned to the Montana pasture. They uncovered seven more nests. All were found in the same layer of sedimentary rock. All were about 23 feet apart. Adult dinosaurs were known to be up to 23 feet long, so that meant that there was just enough room for these big creatures to walk between the nests. Horner realized that the dinosaurs had nested together. He had discovered the first dinosaur nesting colony.

The nests contained mostly crushed and broken shells. The baby dinosaurs in the nests were different sizes. The smallest ones, with no wear on their teeth, were new hatchlings, and the biggest ones showed signs that they had been eating for a while. Horner concluded that the adult dinosaurs were feeding the babies in the nest until they grew big enough to leave. Until Jack Horner's discovery, no one had ever thought that these colony-nesting dinosaurs were also <u>nurturing</u> parents. Horner and Makela called these dinosaurs *Maiasaura peeblesorum*. The *peeblesorum* part was for the Peebles family who owned the pasture where the nests were found. *Maiasura* means "good mother lizard."

Main Idea	1	Answer	Score
	Mark the *main idea*	M	15
	Mark the statement that is *too broad*	B	5
	Mark the statement that is *too narrow*	N	5

a. Dinosaur fossils are found in the American West. ☐ _____

b. The dinosaur nests were about 23 feet apart. ☐ _____

c. Horner and Makela's fossil discovery led to new facts about dinosaur life. ☐ _____

Score 15 points for each correct answer.   Score

Subject Matter   2   This passage is mainly about the
☐ a. discovery of dinosaur nesting colonies.
☐ b. size and shape of hadrosaurs.
☐ c. Peebles family's land.
☐ d. lives of Jack Horner and Bob Makela.   _____

Supporting   3   The dinosaur nests were
Details   ☐ a. 23 feet long.
☐ b. 23 feet apart.
☐ c. on top of the ground.
☐ d. stomped on by adult dinosaurs.   _____

Conclusion   4   This passage leads the reader to conclude that
☐ a. we now know all there is to know about
dinosaurs.
☐ b. we still don't know everything about
dinosaurs.
☐ c. Horner made a lot of money on his discovery.
☐ d. nearly all dinosaurs are found in Montana.   _____

Clarifying   5   The author explains *Maiasaura peeblesorum* by
Devices   ☐ a. telling a story about digging in the rock.
☐ b. relating the history of the Peebles family.
☐ c. telling what each word means.
☐ d. giving reasons why Latin words are used
in naming species.   _____

Vocabulary   6   The word <u>nurturing</u> means
in Context   ☐ a. nervous.
☐ b. caring.
☐ c. curious.
☐ d. nesting.   _____

Add your scores for questions 1–6. Enter the total here   Total
and on the graph on page 159.   Score   _____

36 How Snow Begins

You can roll it, pack it, throw it, and shovel it. You can snowboard and ski on it. But do you know how snow begins?

Snow begins when water vapor or a supercooled droplet of water forms a hexagonal-shaped ice crystal. This crystal forms around a <u>nucleus</u> of a tiny particle that is suspended in the lower atmosphere. These particles might be clay silicate, bits of volcanic ash, or even extraterrestrial material. The ice crystals may fall to the ground in this icy form, as they do in the very cold regions of the Arctic and Antarctic, or they may grow into snow crystals. Snow crystals form by means of sublimation. Sublimation occurs when water vapor turns directly into ice without passing through a liquid stage.

The shape of a snow crystal is determined mostly by temperature and the amount of water vapor present in the air. Two things can happen to falling snow crystals. They can meet with other snow crystals to form aggregations. These are our familiar snowflakes. Or they can meet supercooled water droplets. When this happens, the droplets freeze immediately. The crystals become snow pellets that are called *graupel*.

Have you ever heard that no two snowflakes look exactly alike? This idea probably came from the work of Wilson Alwyn Bentley of Jericho, Vermont. In 1885, Bentley took photographs of snowflakes through a microscope. Thousands of his photomicrographs were collected in a 1931 book titled *Snow Crystals*. Not one of the snowflakes that Bentley photographed was identical to another. No two snowflakes being exactly alike is an interesting idea, but it is difficult to prove.

Main Idea	1		
		Answer	**Score**
Mark the *main idea*		M	15
Mark the statement that is *too broad*		B	5
Mark the statement that is *too narrow*		N	5
a. Snow crystals form aggregations.		☐	_____
b. Snow is all around us.		☐	_____
c. Snow forms in several different ways.		☐	_____

Score 15 points for each correct answer.   **Score**

Subject Matter 2 This passage is mainly about
- [ ] a. what people do with snow.
- [ ] b. how to photograph snow.
- [ ] c. snowfall in the Arctic and Antarctic.
- [ ] d. the formation of snow.

_____

Supporting Details 3 Aggregations of snow crystals are
- [ ] a. ice crystals.
- [ ] b. graupel.
- [ ] c. snowflakes.
- [ ] d. supercooled water droplets.

_____

Conclusion 4 According to the last paragraph, Bentley's photos
- [ ] a. proved that a book about snowflakes could be a commercial success.
- [ ] b. proved that snowflakes could not be photographed.
- [ ] c. did not prove that each snowflake is unique.
- [ ] d. proved that no two snowflakes are alike.

_____

Clarifying Devices 5 The final paragraph of the passage
- [ ] a. continues talking about how snow is formed.
- [ ] b. introduces a new but related topic.
- [ ] c. introduces a new, totally unrelated topic.
- [ ] d. is meant to make the reader laugh.

_____

Vocabulary in Context 6 In this passage, <u>nucleus</u> means
- [ ] a. core.
- [ ] b. starting point.
- [ ] c. stopping point.
- [ ] d. ice cube.

_____

Add your scores for questions 1–6. Enter the total here and on the graph on page 159.   **Total Score**

_____

37 Tracking Down HIV

In the summer of 1980, a patient had a strange purplish spot removed from below his ear. It was Kaposi's sarcoma, a rare form of skin cancer. This patient also had lymph node swelling and exhaustion. In November 1980, a Los Angeles immunologist examined a young man who had diseases linked to immune system malfunctions. The doctor had a T-cell count taken of the patient's blood. T-cells are a type of white blood cell that plays a key role in immune responses. The patient had no helper T-cells.

By the end of 1980, 55 Americans were diagnosed with infections related to immune system breakdown; four had died. A year later the death toll was 74. Intravenous drug users had T-cell abnormalities. People who had received blood transfusions showed symptoms of immune system breakdown. By July 1982, 471 cases of the disease, now called Acquired Immune Deficiency Syndrome (AIDS), had been reported; 184 people had died.

In April 1984, American virologist Dr. Robert Gallo isolated the pathogen, or disease producer, responsible for AIDS. He called it HTLV-III. In Paris, Dr. Luc Montagnier identified a virus he called LAV. An international panel of scientists determined that both men had found the same virus. It became known as Human Immunodeficiency Virus (HIV). Blood banks began screening for HIV in 1985, but by then about 29,000 people had been infected through blood transfusions. Some 12,000 hemophiliacs had contracted HIV through blood-clotting products. By 1995, 477,900 Americans had AIDS; 295,500 had died.

In 1996, researchers announced drugs that reduced HIV in infected people. Today scientists are testing vaccines. They believe that if HIV can be suppressed, then perhaps it can be <u>eradicated</u>, but it is still a race against time.

Main Idea	1		
		Answer	Score
Mark the *main idea*		M	15
Mark the statement that is *too broad*		B	5
Mark the statement that is *too narrow*		N	5
a. Drugs seem able to suppress HIV.		☐	_____
b. The history of HIV spans 20 years.		☐	_____
c. A virus can be deadly.		☐	_____

Score 15 points for each correct answer.   **Score**

Subject Matter   **2**   This passage is mainly about
- ☐ a. the spreading of the disease known as HIV.
- ☐ b. the work of Dr. Robert Gallo.
- ☐ c. infectious diseases.
- ☐ d. the symptoms of HIV.

            _____

Supporting Details   **3**   A T-cell is a
- ☐ a. patient's blood.
- ☐ b. deadly strain of tuberculosis.
- ☐ c. white blood cell important in providing immunity to disease.
- ☐ d. red blood cell.

            _____

Conclusion   **4**   The final paragraph leads the reader to see that scientists
- ☐ a. have no hope in ever finding a cure for HIV.
- ☐ b. have hope that a cure for HIV will be found.
- ☐ c. have run out of time to find a cure for HIV.
- ☐ d. are in a contest against one another to find a cure for HIV.

            _____

Clarifying Devices   **5**   The basic pattern used to develop this passage is
- ☐ a. chronological order.
- ☐ b. personal narrative.
- ☐ c. comparison and contrast.
- ☐ d. question and answer.

            _____

Vocabulary in Context   **6**   The word <u>eradicated</u> means
- ☐ a. made extreme.
- ☐ b. celebrated.
- ☐ c. remove by rubbing.
- ☐ d. gotten rid of entirely.

            _____

Add your scores for questions 1–6. Enter the total here and on the graph on page 159.   **Total Score**   _____

38 Chemical Compounds

Scientists have identified more than 100 chemical elements. The atoms of each element are unique. All the matter in the universe is composed of the atoms of these elements. A sample of any pure element has only atoms that are characteristic of that element. For example, the atoms that make up the element carbon are different from the atoms that make up the element iron, and those atoms are different from the atoms that make up the element gold. Each element has its own symbol consisting of one, two, or three letters. The letters come from either the current name of the element, such as C, H, and O for carbon, hydrogen, and oxygen, or from the original name of the element. The original name is often its Latin name; for example, Fe is the symbol for iron, which had an original Latin name of *ferrum*.

Elements also combine with other elements to make chemical compounds. The atoms of the elements are like letters of the alphabet. Just as letters can be combined to form words, the atoms of the elements can combine to form many different compounds. The <u>formula</u> of a compound tells the types and the ratios of the atoms present in the compound. For example, water is a chemical compound of the elements of hydrogen and oxygen. The atoms are in the ratio of two hydrogen atoms for every oxygen atom. The formula for water is written H_2O. Methane is a chemical compound formed from the elements carbon and hydrogen. There are four hydrogen atoms for each single carbon atom. The formula for methane is written CH_4.

There are millions of known chemical compounds, and there are many more millions that have not yet been discovered.

Main Idea	1		
		Answer	**Score**
	Mark the *main idea*	M	15
	Mark the statement that is *too broad*	B	5
	Mark the statement that is *too narrow*	N	5
	a. There are more than 100 different chemical elements.	☐	_____
	b. Chemical elements and compounds are named in specific ways.	☐	_____
	c. Matter is made of elements.	☐	_____

Score 15 points for each correct answer.   **Score**

Subject Matter   **2**   This passage deals mainly with
☐ a. the more than 100 different elements.
☐ b. atoms.
☐ c. how elements and compounds are named.
☐ d. the formula for water.   _____

Supporting Details   **3**   The formula for methane, CH4, stands for
☐ a. a total of four atoms.
☐ b. one carbon atom and four hydrogen atoms.
☐ c. four carbon atoms and one hydrogen atom.
☐ d. four carbon atoms and four hydrogen atoms.   _____

Conclusion   **4**   This passage leads the reader to conclude that
☐ a. all chemical compounds contain carbon.
☐ b. there are exactly one million chemical compounds.
☐ c. the search for chemical compounds is ongoing.
☐ d. all chemical compounds have been discovered.   _____

Clarifying Devices   **5**   In the second paragraph, the statement that "atoms . . . are like letters of the alphabet" is
☐ a. a simile.
☐ b. a metaphor.
☐ c. personification.
☐ d. an exaggeration.   _____

Vocabulary in Context   **6**   In this passage, the word <u>formula</u> means
☐ a. a statement of religious belief.
☐ b. a mixture fed to babies.
☐ c. the symbols that express a compound.
☐ d. a plan or method.   _____

Add your scores for questions 1–6. Enter the total here and on the graph on page 159.   **Total Score**   _____

39 Whatever Floats Your Boat

There is a story that cannot be proven about the Greek mathematician and inventor Archimedes. Supposedly Archimedes was in his bath way back in the third century B.C. when he noted the level of the bath water rising as he submerged himself. It is said that he leaped from his bath and ran naked through the streets crying "Eureka!" which in English means "I have found it." What had gotten Archimedes so excited became known as Archimedes' principle. This law of physics states that any object floating upon or submerged in a fluid is <u>buoyed</u> upward by a force equal to the weight of the displaced fluid.

What does that mean in real-life terms? In fact, Archimedes' principle is the basis of naval architecture. A ship launched into the ocean will sink until the weight of the water it displaces, or pushes out of the way, is equal to the ship's own weight. A ship is designed to carry fuel, lubricating oil, crew, and crew supplies to operate. This weight is called deadweight. Added to the deadweight is the weight of the ship's structure and machinery. This is known as lightship weight. The sum of deadweight and lightship weight is displacement—that is, the weight that must be equaled by the weight of displaced water if the ship is to float. A cargo ship must also be designed to carry a specified weight of cargo, because as the ship is loaded with cargo, it will sink deeper, displacing more water.

Naval architects use formulas to approximate the various weights needed to be figured into a ship's design. These experience-based formulas usually produce accurate predictions of the ship's draft—that is, the depth of water in which the finished ship will float. Like Archimedes, the naval architect can cry "Eureka!" when he or she has found the size of the ship that the sum of all weights requires.

Main Idea	1		
		Answer	**Score**
	Mark the *main idea*	M	15
	Mark the statement that is *too broad*	B	5
	Mark the statement that is *too narrow*	N	5

a. Archimedes' principle about water displacement is vital to shipbuilding. ☐ _____

b. Archimedes supposedly cried "Eureka!" ☐ _____

c. All ships displace water. ☐ _____

Score 15 points for each correct answer. **Score**

Subject Matter   **2**   This passage is mainly about
- [ ] a. the life of Archimedes.
- [ ] b. cargo ships.
- [ ] c. the laws of physics.
- [ ] d. Archimedes' principle and its effects on naval architecture.

                                                   _____

Supporting
Details   **3**   A ship will sink until
- [ ] a. fuel, oil, crew, and supplies are removed.
- [ ] b. the water covers its cargo.
- [ ] c. the weight of the water it displaces is equal to its own weight.
- [ ] d. a naval architect supervises its loading.

                                                   _____

Conclusion   **4**   Before Archimedes' principle, ship captains were
- [ ] a. never exactly sure how much weight they could safely carry.
- [ ] b. anxious to sail to faraway ports.
- [ ] c. interested only in sailing heavyweight boats.
- [ ] d. sure that sea monsters moved ocean waters.

                                                   _____

Clarifying
Devices   **5**   Which phrase defines the draft of a ship?
- [ ] a. experience-based formulas
- [ ] b. depth of water in which the finished ship will float
- [ ] c. the size of the ship
- [ ] d. approximate the various weights

                                                   _____

Vocabulary
in Context   **6**   In this passage, <u>buoyed</u> means
- [ ] a. destroyed by water.
- [ ] b. built by a naval architect.
- [ ] c. held up or kept from sinking.
- [ ] d. made to feel excited or happy.

                                                   _____

Add your scores for questions 1–6. Enter the total here
and on the graph on page 159.
     Total
     Score   _____

40 A Malaria-Carrying Mosquito

First come the shakes, the fever, the burning throat. Next are the chills. Your pulse rate <u>plummets</u>, and a drenching sweat ices you from head to toe. Your face turns pale, and your nails turn blue. Then you either cough up thick black blood and die—or you survive. If you survive, depression might hang on for months. Finally, you're afraid the symptoms may strike again. You've had the tropical disease *malaria*.

In 1904, the United States began building a canal through the Isthmus of Panama, but canal workers were getting sick and many were dying. That was because conditions in Panama were ideal for breeding the female *Anopheles*, a malaria-carrying mosquito. The females lay eggs in standing water in rain barrels, storage jars, and thousands of puddles. Larvae, called *wrigglers,* hatch from the eggs and develop into adult mosquitoes. When the mosquitoes suck the blood of a person infected with malaria, the deadly parasites breed in the mosquitoes' stomachs and migrate to their salivary glands. After that, every person the mosquitoes bite gets a dose of deadly parasites. Infected victims transmit parasites to other mosquitoes that bite them, and these mosquitoes in turn infect other people. Unchecked, cases of malaria rise to epidemic proportions.

To eliminate mosquito breeding grounds in Panama, swamps were filled with dirt or drained dry. Other watery areas were coated with oil and larvicide. Surface-feeding fish, spiders, and lizards were put into rivers and fields to eat adult mosquitoes. Even human mosquito-catchers were paid 10 cents an hour to swat the deadly insects.

Malaria was never entirely eradicated, but it was reduced from infecting 82 percent of canal workers in 1906 to infecting less than eight percent in 1913 when the Panama Canal was completed.

Main Idea	1		
		Answer	Score
	Mark the *main idea*	M	15
	Mark the statement that is *too broad*	B	5
	Mark the statement that is *too narrow*	N	5

a. Tropical diseases are found in Panama. ☐ _____

b. Controlling the *Anopheles* mosquito helped the builders of the Panama Canal. ☐ _____

c. Malaria causes the chills. ☐ _____

Score 15 points for each correct answer.   **Score**

Subject Matter   2   This passage is mainly about
    ☐ a. the fight against a tropical disease.
    ☐ b. insects.
    ☐ c. building the Panama Canal.
    ☐ d. canal workers in Panama.
_____

Supporting Details   3   To lay their eggs, female *Anopheles* need
    ☐ a. deadly parasites.
    ☐ b. wrigglers.
    ☐ c. standing water.
    ☐ d. larvicide.
_____

Conclusion   4   Without the mosquito-control efforts,
    ☐ a. there would have been war in Panama.
    ☐ b. the Panama Canal may never have been completed.
    ☐ c. cities would have been built along the canal.
    ☐ d. spiders and lizards would have died.
_____

Clarifying Devices   5   In the second paragraph, *Anopheles* is
    ☐ a. the name of a kind of mosquito.
    ☐ b. the title of a book about mosquitoes.
    ☐ c. a Panamanian expression.
    ☐ d. an emphasized word.
_____

Vocabulary in Context   6   The word <u>plummets</u> means
    ☐ a. drops rapidly.
    ☐ b. resembles a smallish purple fruit.
    ☐ c. heats up.
    ☐ d. resembles a hammer.
_____

Add your scores for questions 1–6. Enter the total here and on the graph on page 159.   **Total Score**   _____

41 Carbon Is Everywhere

Carbon is the major component of many minerals. Carbon compounds form the common minerals magnesite, dolomite, marble, and limestone. Coral and the shells of oysters and clams are mainly calcium carbonate. Carbon is also in coal and in the organic compounds that make up petroleum, natural gas, and all plant and animal tissue.

Diamond, the hardest known natural substance, is pure carbon. The word *diamond* comes from the Greek word *adamas,* meaning "the invincible," a term that accurately describes a diamond's permanence. The properties of a diamond are derived from its crystal structure of interlocking four-sided carbon atoms. Each carbon atom is linked to four <u>equidistant</u> neighbors throughout the crystal. The hardness, brilliance, and sparkle of diamond makes it unsurpassed as a gemstone. Diamond is also ideal for industrial applications, such as drilling oil wells and boring tunnels in solid rock.

Graphite, a very different substance, is the other crystal form of carbon. Its name is derived from the Greek verb *graphein,* which means "to write." This name refers to the fact that graphite leaves a dark mark when it is rubbed on a surface. Graphite is a lustrous black substance that easily crumbles or flakes. Its slippery feel is caused by its breaking from the crystal in thin layers. Graphite is composed entirely of planes of three-sided carbon atoms joined in a honeycomb pattern. Each carbon molecule is bonded to three others. One of the main uses for graphite is as a lubricant. A familiar use is as the "lead" in pencils.

Carbon, the sixth most abundant element in the universe, deserves to be called the most versatile known element.

Main Idea	1	Answer	Score
	Mark the *main idea*	M	15
	Mark the statement that is *too broad*	B	5
	Mark the statement that is *too narrow*	N	5

a. Carbon is an abundant, versatile element found in many substances. ☐ _____

b. Carbon is a chemical element. ☐ _____

c. Graphite is one of the crystal forms of carbon. ☐ _____

Subject Matter **2** This passage is mainly about
- [ ] a. the properties of graphite.
- [ ] b. familiar minerals and compounds in which carbon is found.
- [ ] c. the properties of minerals.
- [ ] d. crystal structures.   _____

Supporting Details **3** Calcium carbonate is present in
- [ ] a. coral.
- [ ] b. natural gas.
- [ ] c. marble.
- [ ] d. lead.   _____

Conclusion **4** Diamond is used in industrial applications because of its
- [ ] a. availability.
- [ ] b. sparkle.
- [ ] c. brilliance.
- [ ] d. hardness.   _____

Clarifying Devices **5** The phrases in quotations, "the invincible" and "to write," are
- [ ] a. Greek words.
- [ ] b. definitions of Greek words.
- [ ] c. key words in this passage.
- [ ] d. quoted words from Greek scientists.   _____

Vocabulary in Context **6** The word <u>equidistant</u> means
- [ ] a. equally separated.
- [ ] b. interlocking.
- [ ] c. not close together.
- [ ] d. on the equator.   _____

Add your scores for questions 1–6. Enter the total here and on the graph on page 159.   **Total Score**   _____

42 Newton's Laws of Motion

Isaac Newton, while a student at Cambridge, showed no particular scientific talent. When the plague closed the university in 1665, Newton returned home to Lincolnshire, England. There he continued his studies on his own, and there his genius emerged. Within 18 months after leaving Cambridge, he made <u>revolutionary</u> advances in mathematics, optics, physics, and astronomy. He began a lifetime of scientific work that had tremendous influence on modern science. His three laws of motion form the foundation for all interactions of force, matter, and motion. He published these laws in 1686 in his book *Principia Mathematica.*

Newton's first law is that if a body (anything with mass) is at rest or moving at a constant speed in a straight line, it will remain at rest or keep moving in a straight line at constant speed unless it is acted upon by a force. This is the law of inertia. Prior to the 17th century, it was thought that bodies could move only as long as a force acted on them; they would remain at rest if no force moved them. Newton's first law helped scientists realize that no force was needed to keep the planets moving in their orbits.

Newton's second law states that the larger the force, the larger the acceleration; and the larger the mass, the smaller the acceleration. This law helps explain why if the same force is exerted on two objects, the lighter object will accelerate more quickly.

Newton's third law postulates that the actions of two bodies upon each other are always equal and directly opposite; that is, reaction is always equal and opposite to action. For example, the downward force of a book lying on a table is equal to the upward force of the table on the book. This law of motion is particularly relevant when considering gravitational forces—a flying airplane pulls up on the earth with the same force that the earth pulls down on the airplane.

Main Idea 1

	Answer	Score
Mark the *main idea*	M	15
Mark the statement that is *too broad*	B	5
Mark the statement that is *too narrow*	N	5

a. Isaac Newton was a student at Cambridge University. ☐ _____

b. Isaac Newton contributed to science. ☐ _____

c. Isaac Newton formulated the three laws of motion. ☐ _____

Subject Matter **2** The passage is mostly about
- [ ] a. Newton's laws of motion.
- [ ] b. Newton's education.
- [ ] c. the work habits of scientists.
- [ ] d. why planets stay in their orbits.   _____

Supporting Details **3** Newton's first law of motion helped 17th-century scientists understand
- [ ] a. velocity.
- [ ] b. the orbits of planets.
- [ ] c. acceleration.
- [ ] d. inertia.   _____

Conclusion **4** From reading about Newton's early life, one can conclude that he
- [ ] a. learned more in school than on his own.
- [ ] b. was most successful when working independently.
- [ ] c. thought he had great teachers at Cambridge.
- [ ] d. wanted to start his own school.   _____

Clarifying Devices **5** The second through fourth paragraphs
- [ ] a. explain each of Newton's laws.
- [ ] b. give a brief biography of Newton.
- [ ] c. sum up Newton's lifetime of work.
- [ ] d. explain mathematics, optics, and physics.   _____

Vocabulary in Context **6** In this passage, <u>revolutionary</u> means
- [ ] a. having to do with wars for freedom.
- [ ] b. spinning in a circle.
- [ ] c. new and surprising.
- [ ] d. orbiting around the sun.   _____

Add your scores for questions 1–6. Enter the total here and on the graph on page 159.   **Total Score**   _____

43 Mr. Jefferson's Moose

Thomas Jefferson—author of the Declaration of Independence, statesman, architect, inventor, and scientist—was offended when he read the inaccurate reporting of a French naturalist, Count Georges de Buffon. Buffon had written in *Histoire Naturelle* (*Natural History*) that the United States was one big gloomy swamp inhabited by weak and tiny animals. Jefferson, who was both a dedicated naturalist and a patriot, vowed to set the French count straight. Jefferson's opportunity came in 1784 when the U.S. Congress asked him to serve as a diplomat in Paris.

When in Paris, Jefferson asked to meet Buffon. They were introduced at a party. Jefferson began to tell him about the very large animals in America. One animal he mentioned was the American moose, so huge that the antlers of a European reindeer walking under it would not touch its belly. Jefferson's story was rudely interrupted by laughter. Buffon thought this was the silliest thing he had ever heard. Jefferson decided to provide proof. He wrote to his friend Governor John Sullivan of New Hampshire and asked him to ship him the biggest moose in the North Woods. Eagerly Sullivan and a group of men <u>trekked</u> deep into the woods until they found, trapped, and killed a giant seven-foot moose. Sullivan had the moose stuffed, packed in a crate, and shipped to France.

Everyone gathered around as the crate was opened in Paris. Inside was the biggest moose any of them had ever seen! It was not exactly pretty, as most of its hair had fallen out. But with the hairless moose towering over him, Buffon admitted his error. He promised that in his next book he would revise his statements about animal life in North America.

Main Idea	1	Answer	Score
	Mark the *main idea*	M	15
	Mark the statement that is *too broad*	B	5
	Mark the statement that is *too narrow*	N	5
	a. Thomas Jefferson knew about nature.	☐	_____
	b. Thomas Jefferson's stuffed moose proved a scientific point.	☐	_____
	c. Thomas Jefferson had a moose shipped to him in Paris.	☐	_____

Subject Matter   **2**   This passage is mostly about
- ☐ a. the animals of North America.
- ☐ b. French scientific studies.
- ☐ c. hunting in New Hampshire.
- ☐ d. how Thomas Jefferson made his case about American animals.   _____

Supporting Details   **3**   At a party in Paris, Jefferson described
- ☐ a. the silliest thing he had ever seen.
- ☐ b. a French reindeer.
- ☐ c. the size of an American moose.
- ☐ d. a moose's belly.   _____

Conclusion   **4**   The moose sent to Jefferson in Paris provided
- ☐ a. visual scientific evidence.
- ☐ b. oral scientific evidence.
- ☐ c. a scientific theory.
- ☐ d. a lot of laughs for the French scientists.   _____

Clarifying Devices   **5**   In the first paragraph, *Histoire Naturelle*
- ☐ a. is the name of a naturalist.
- ☐ b. is the title of a book.
- ☐ c. is an old French expression.
- ☐ d. was Buffon's name for America.   _____

Vocabulary in Context   **6**   The word <u>trekked</u> means
- ☐ a. hid.
- ☐ b. illegally walked on someone else's land.
- ☐ c. knocked down trees.
- ☐ d. traveled.   _____

Add your scores for questions 1–6. Enter the total here and on the graph on page 159.   **Total Score**   _____

44 Cryosurgery

Have you ever heard of cryosurgery? It is a procedure in which abnormal body tissues (sometimes referred to as *lesions*) are destroyed by exposing them to extremely cold temperatures. The temperatures used range from −150°C (−238°F) to absolute zero (−273°C or −460°F). The surgical procedure freezes unhealthy tissue, and the freezing destroys the cells. For external lesions, liquid nitrogen, which has a temperature of −196°C (−320.8°F), is applied directly to the cells. For internal tumors, liquid nitrogen is circulated through an instrument called a *cryoprobe,* a low-temperature scalpel or probe cooled by liquid nitrogen.

How does cryosurgery destroy cells? The intracellular ice created by the liquid nitrogen will destroy nearly all cells it comes in contact with. As ice forms around a cell, the free water inside the cell is drawn off. This causes the cell to shrink and the walls or membranes inside the cell to collapse. Toxic proteins or chemicals within the cell are released. Finally, as the ice around shrunken cells begins to thaw, large amounts of free water rush back inside the cells, causing them to burst. The dead cells are then removed through normal bodily processes.

How well does cryosurgery work? The procedure has proved successful in removing tonsils, hemorrhoids, warts, cataracts, and some tumors. Cryosurgery may be used as well to remove freckles (for cosmetic reasons) and to treat some skin cancers. It is also used in the treatment of bone cancer to freeze internal bone <u>cavities</u>. Cryosurgery has evolved from the first attempts to freeze tissue with a salt-ice mixture in the 1850s to the sophisticated cryoprobe method used today.

Main Idea	1		Answer	Score
		Mark the *main idea*	M	15
		Mark the statement that is *too broad*	B	5
		Mark the statement that is *too narrow*	N	5

a. Cryosurgery is used to treat patients. ☐ _____

b. Cryosurgery is used in the treatment of some skin cancers. ☐ _____

c. Cryosurgery is used in the treatment of abnormal tissue. ☐ _____

Score 15 points for each correct answer.   Score

Subject Matter **2** This passage is mainly about
☐ a. the medical procedure of cryosurgery.
☐ b. the structure of unhealthy cells.
☐ c. the advantages and disadvantages of
cryosurgery.
☐ d. cancer treatments.   _____

Supporting **3** The temperatures used in cryosurgery range from
Details
☐ a. −196°C to −320.8°F.
☐ b. −150°C to absolute zero (−273°C).
☐ c. the intracellular to the intercellular.
☐ d. −150°C to −238°F.   _____

Conclusion **4** Medical interest in cryosurgery began
☐ a. thousands of years ago.
☐ b. in the last 20 years.
☐ c. more than a century ago.
☐ d. in the 1990s.   _____

Clarifying **5** The overall structure of this passage is
Devices
☐ a. a personal narrative.
☐ b. cause and effect.
☐ c. steps in a process.
☐ d. question and answer.   _____

Vocabulary **6** As used in this passage, <u>cavities</u> are
in Context
☐ a. holes in teeth.
☐ b. taking place between the stars.
☐ c. hollow places.
☐ d. happening outside the walls of a cell.   _____

Add your scores for questions 1–6. Enter the total here Total
and on the graph on page 159.   Score   _____

45 Hurricanes

Hurricanes were named long ago by a Caribbean island people who blamed the devastating storms on Huracan, their god of evil. In Australia, hurricanes are called *cyclones* or *willy-willies;* in India they are *typhoons;* in parts of Mexico, they are called *cordonazo,* "lash of a whip."

Hurricanes form over tropical oceans when high surface water temperatures (about 80ºF) cause the evaporation of massive quantities of water. This provides the tropical atmosphere with a rich supply of water vapor. The moist air is carried aloft where it condenses and releases latent heat. This warming strengthens the updraft, creating a low-pressure area in the lower atmosphere. Surrounding air moves into this low-pressure region, which in turn provides more energy from the condensation of even more lifted water vapor. Another ingredient in the formation of hurricanes is the <u>convergence</u> of winds blowing from different directions. These winds collide and create a pileup of air. The air at the center of the collision moves upward, becoming an updraft.

Rising air and convergence create ordinary thunderstorms, but as more hot updrafts rise into the storms, the clouds grow larger. Several thunderstorms might cluster together to become a tropical disturbance, the first stage in hurricane formation. The next stage occurs when the developing thunderstorm cluster begins to swirl, a movement caused by the rotation of the earth. When swirling winds reach sustained speeds of 23 miles per hour, the disturbance is called a tropical depression. When wind speeds reach 40 miles per hour, it is called a tropical storm. At 74 miles per hour, it is called a hurricane. Hurricanes last approximately five to seven days. When they cross land or cool ocean water, they lose their oceanic moisture source, and their energy-providing latent heat decreases. The storm loses intensity and dies out.

Main Idea	1		
		Answer	**Score**
	Mark the *main idea*	M	15
	Mark the statement that is *too broad*	B	5
	Mark the statement that is *too narrow*	N	5
	a. Hurricanes form over warm oceans.	☐	____
	b. Many storms form over warm oceans.	☐	____
	c. Moist air rises over warm oceans.	☐	____

Score 15 points for each correct answer.   **Score**

Subject Matter   **2**   This passage is mainly about
        ☐ a. how hurricanes got their names.
        ☐ b. the dangers of hurricanes.
        ☐ c. storm safety.
        ☐ d. the formation of hurricanes.   _____

Supporting   **3**   When wind speeds of a disturbance reach
Details   74 miles an hour, the storm is called
        ☐ a. an ordinary thunderstorm.
        ☐ b. a tropical storm.
        ☐ c. a hurricane.
        ☐ d. a tropical depression.   _____

Conclusion   **4**   Over which of the following would a hurricane
      most likely *not* lose strength?
        ☐ a. Mexico
        ☐ b. a tropical sea
        ☐ c. the east coast of the United States
        ☐ d. the cold north Atlantic Ocean   _____

Clarifying   **5**   The information in this passage is mainly
Devices   presented through
        ☐ a. a historical perspective.
        ☐ b. a personal narrative.
        ☐ c. an explanation of a process.
        ☐ d. a descriptive account.   _____

Vocabulary   **6**   The word <u>convergence</u> means
in Context   ☐ a. the act of coming together.
        ☐ b. clouds that produce rain and thunder.
        ☐ c. the process of water vapor changing into
           liquid.
        ☐ d. an updraft.   _____

Add your scores for questions 1–6. Enter the total here   **Total**
and on the graph on page 159.   **Score**   _____

46 Kinds of Rock

Rock, the hard, solid part of the earth, can be grouped by its mineral content, by its appearance, and even by the way it is used. But the most common way to classify rocks is to group them by the way they are formed. According to this method of classification, there are three main kinds of rocks.

Igneous. The word *igneous* means "having to do with fire." Igneous rocks form from magma—molten material—that reaches the earth's surface as lava or that cools and solidifies within the earth's crust before reaching the surface. Examples of igneous rocks are glassy obsidian, porous pumice, the finely crystalline rocks of basalt and felsite, and the coarsely crystalline rocks of granite and gabbros.

Sedimentary. Sedimentary rocks form when particles that have eroded from other rocks of all kinds are buried. Sedimentary rocks also come from other rocks and minerals that have dissolved in ocean water. The particles, or sediments, become hard and <u>compact</u>. Over long periods of time, they turn into sedimentary rocks. The size, shape, and chemical nature of the particles determine the kind of rock the particles become. Examples of sedimentary rocks are sandstone, shale, and limestone.

Metamorphic. These rocks get their name from the Greek words *meta* and *morphe,* which together mean "change of form." Metamorphic rocks are igneous or sedimentary rocks that have been altered by great pressure or temperature. In some metamorphic rocks, new minerals are formed and the appearance of the rock changes greatly. This happens when the calcite in limestone recrystallizes to form marble and when the quartz grains in sandstone grow larger to form the connecting crystals of quartzite.

Main Idea	1	Answer	Score
	Mark the *main idea*	M	15
	Mark the statement that is *too broad*	B	5
	Mark the statement that is *too narrow*	N	5
	a. Rocks are the solid part of the earth.	☐	____
	b. Rocks can be classified by the way they are formed.	☐	____
	c. Metamorphic rocks may be igneous rocks that have been altered.	☐	____

Subject Matter   **2**   This passage is mostly about
  - ☐ a. why rock is categorized in different ways.
  - ☐ b. Greek words meaning "rock."
  - ☐ c. characteristics of the three main kinds of rocks.
  - ☐ d. grouping rocks by their mineral content.   _____

Supporting Details   **3**   Igneous rocks come from
  - ☐ a. cooled magma.
  - ☐ b. layers of sediment at the bottom of the oceans.
  - ☐ c. rocks under great pressure.
  - ☐ d. sandstone crystals.   _____

Conclusion   **4**   It seems likely that rock formation happens
  - ☐ a. only on land.
  - ☐ b. only in water.
  - ☐ c. over a long period of time.
  - ☐ d. quite quickly.   _____

Clarifying Devices   **5**   The subheads in bold type are the three kinds of
  - ☐ a. rock.
  - ☐ b. crystals.
  - ☐ c. Greek words.
  - ☐ d. minerals.   _____

Vocabulary in Context   **6**   In this passage, <u>compact</u> means
  - ☐ a. small or miniature.
  - ☐ b. a contract or agreement.
  - ☐ c. of a beautiful and high quality.
  - ☐ d. firmly packed together.   _____

Add your scores for questions 1–6. Enter the total here and on the graph on page 159.   **Total Score**   _____

47 Endangered Amphibians

Amphibians are the only group of animals on the earth that spend part of their lives on land and part in the water. Worldwide the amphibian population—that is, the number of creatures such as frogs, toads, and salamanders—is <u>declining</u>. Among the possible causes for this phenomenon is pollution. Scientific data strongly suggest that certain kinds of pollution are at least partially responsible. One of the sources of pollution is acid precipitation.

Acid rain and snow can affect amphibians in remote places that seem free of human activity. Precipitation in the air mixes with pollutants, such as sulfur and nitrate from automobile exhaust and coal-burning factories, to produce sulfuric acid and nitric acid. Acid precipitation can be devastating to life.

The acid from precipitation accumulates in and around lakes and ponds where amphibians live. Concentrations of acid are highest in early spring. This puts newly laid amphibian eggs at risk. Melting acid snow can produce an acid pulse, which is a sudden release of acid into the water. It acts like a dose of poison. Studies show that even slightly acidic water can kill the eggs of frogs and toads or cause deformed tadpoles. Acid precipitation has been blamed for the disappearance of tiger salamanders from parts of the Colorado Rockies.

Some amphibian species, such as the New Jersey Pine Barrens frog, thrive in water with high acid content. Scientists offer an explanation for this exception: because the level of acid has been the same for many years, the frogs have managed to adapt to conditions that would kill other species. Amphibians are highly adaptable, but they need time to adapt to new conditions. Human-made changes, such as acid pulses, can be deadly.

Main Idea	1		Answer	Score
	Mark the *main idea*		M	15
	Mark the statement that is *too broad*		B	5
	Mark the statement that is *too narrow*		N	5
	a. Acid rain can cause deformed tadpoles.		☐	___
	b. There are fewer amphibians around.		☐	___
	c. Acid rain may be causing the amphibian population to decrease.		☐	___

Subject Matter   **2**   This passage is mainly about
- ☐ a. how amphibians grow.
- ☐ b. precipitation.
- ☐ c. pollution's effect on lakes and ponds.
- ☐ d. pollution's effect on amphibians.   _____

Supporting Details   **3**   Acidic water can
- ☐ a. melt snow.
- ☐ b. cause rain to fall.
- ☐ c. kill amphibian eggs.
- ☐ d. accelerate the pulse of a frog.   _____

Conclusion   **4**   Which statement is probably true about amphibians?
- ☐ a. They may adapt to certain kinds of pollutants.
- ☐ b. They need acid rain to survive.
- ☐ c. They are found only in isolated areas.
- ☐ d. They lay their eggs in late summer.   _____

Clarifying Devices   **5**   The structure of this passage is
- ☐ a. chronological.
- ☐ b. narrative.
- ☐ c. cause and effect.
- ☐ d. question and answer.   _____

Vocabulary in Context   **6**   In this passage, <u>declining</u> means
- ☐ a. arguing.
- ☐ b. absorbing.
- ☐ c. lessening.
- ☐ d. increasing.   _____

Add your scores for questions 1–6. Enter the total here and on the graph on page 159.   **Total Score**   _____

48 Come In. It's COOL Inside!

It may be difficult to imagine a movie theater today that wouldn't be cool on a hot day, but air-conditioned comfort was once a big bonus for your ticket price. In fact, circulating conditioned air, fed into the theater from the ceiling and taken out from the floor level, was first installed in 1922 at Graumann's Metropolitan Theater in Los Angeles, California.

Willis Carrier invented a mechanical air conditioner in 1911. With the development of Freons in the early 1930s, air-conditioning systems began to be installed in office buildings, hospitals, apartments, trains, and buses. Freons are highly efficient refrigerant gases that are carbon compounds containing fluorine and chlorine or bromine. The refrigerant becomes a liquid and gives off heat when it is <u>compressed</u>. When the pressure is removed, it becomes a gas that absorbs heat.

In the air-cooling cycle, warm humid air is drawn from the room and forced over the cooling coil that contains the refrigerant. The warm air gives up its heat to the refrigerant. The refrigerant fluid vaporizes as it absorbs the heat in the air. The moisture in the cooled air condenses on fins over the coils, and the water runs down the fins and drains out. The cooled dehumidified air is blown back into the room.

Meanwhile, the vaporized and now much warmer refrigerant moves to the compressor. The compressor pumps it under pressure to the condenser coils. Here the heat in the refrigerant is transferred outside by fan. The refrigerant is recirculated to the cooling coil as a liquid to continue the cooling process. A thermostat controls the compressor motor, turning it off when the room temperature is cool enough and restarting it as the temperature begins to rise. As for the movie-going audience, all they have to do is enjoy the movie as the air conditioner keeps them cool.

Main Idea	1	Answer	Score
Mark the *main idea*		M	15
Mark the statement that is *too broad*		B	5
Mark the statement that is *too narrow*		N	5

a. Air conditioning keeps people cool. ☐ _____

b. Freons are refrigerants. ☐ _____

c. The air conditioning process uses refrigerant gases to remove heat from the air. ☐ _____

Subject Matter   **2**   This passage is mainly about
☐ a. movie theaters.
☐ b. the development of Freons.
☐ c. how air conditioners work.
☐ d. compressors and thermostats.   _____

Supporting Details   **3**   Air conditioners began to be installed in office buildings in the
☐ a. 1920s.
☐ b. 1910s.
☐ c. 1950s.
☐ d. 1930s.   _____

Conclusion   **4**   The development of Freons was important to the development of
☐ a. large-scale air conditioning.
☐ b. office buildings.
☐ c. carbon compounds.
☐ d. movie theaters.   _____

Clarifying Devices   **5**   In the fourth paragraph, the word *meanwhile* indicates that the process is happening
☐ a. at the same time the cooled air is blown into the room.
☐ b. after the cooled air is blown into the room.
☐ c. before the cooled air is blown into the room.
☐ d. in another series of machines.   _____

Vocabulary in Context   **6**   In this passage, <u>compressed</u> means
☐ a. frozen.
☐ b. squeezed together by pressure.
☐ c. exploded.
☐ d. complicated.   _____

Add your scores for questions 1–6. Enter the total here and on the graph on page 159.   **Total Score**   _____

97

49 Can You Hear This?

When something creates a sound wave in a room or an auditorium, listeners hear the sound wave directly from the source. They also hear the reflections as the sound bounces off the walls, floor, and ceiling. These sounds, called the *reflected wave* or *reverberant sound,* can be heard even after the sound is no longer coming from the source.

The reverberation time of an auditorium is determined by the volume or interior size of the auditorium. It is also determined by how well or how poorly the walls, ceiling, floor, and contents of the room (including the people) absorb sound. There is no ideal reverberation time, because each use of an auditorium calls for different reverberation. Speech needs to be understood clearly; therefore rooms used for talking must have a short reverberation time. The full-sound performance of music such as Wagner operas or Mahler symphonies should have a long reverberation time. The light, rapid musical passages of Bach or Mozart need a reverberation time somewhere between.

Acoustic problems often are caused by poor auditorium design. Smooth, curved reflecting surfaces, such as domes and curved walls, create large echoes. Parallel walls reflect sound back and forth, creating a rapid, repetitive pulsing effect. Large pillars, corners, and low balconies can cause acoustic shadows as the sound waves try to pass around the obstacles. Some of these problems can be lessened by using absorbers and reflectors to change the reverberation time of a room. For example, hanging large reflectors, called clouds, over the performers will allow some sound frequencies to reflect and others to pass to achieve a pleasing mixture of sound.

Main Idea 1	Answer	Score
Mark the *main idea*	M	15
Mark the statement that is *too broad*	B	5
Mark the statement that is *too narrow*	N	5
a. Listeners hear sound waves.	☐	____
b. Various factors must be considered to get good sound in auditoriums.	☐	____
c. Parallel walls make sound bounce back and forth.	☐	____

Subject Matter   2   This passage is mainly about
- [ ] a. how the sound of speech differs from the sound of music.
- [ ] b. the types of music orchestras play.
- [ ] c. why auditoriums shouldn't have curved walls.
- [ ] d. how auditoriums should be designed to account for sound waves.   ____

Supporting Details   3   Opera music sounds fuller in an auditorium with
- [ ] a. long reverberation time.
- [ ] b. short reverberation time.
- [ ] c. intermediate reverberation time.
- [ ] d. no reverberation time.   ____

Conclusion   4   This passage suggests that the goal of good auditorium design is to
- [ ] a. achieve a pleasing mixture of sound.
- [ ] b. get rid of all echoes.
- [ ] c. make sure sound is not too loud.
- [ ] d. make auditoriums larger.   ____

Clarifying Devices   5   Large pillars and low balconies
- [ ] a. make sound rich and full.
- [ ] b. are cures for sound problems.
- [ ] c. are sources of sound problems.
- [ ] d. work the same as clouds.   ____

Vocabulary in Context   6   Acoustic means
- [ ] a. located in a large open room.
- [ ] b. having to do with music.
- [ ] c. having to do with sound.
- [ ] d. overwhelming.   ____

Add your scores for questions 1–6. Enter the total here and on the graph on page 159.   Total Score   ____

50 Genetic Engineering

Genetic engineering began when the DNA molecule, the most basic unit of life, was first described in 1953 by James Watson and Francis Crick. An understanding of DNA led to the altering of normal cell reproduction. Experiments with altering human cells began in 1970. In one of the first experiments, patients were injected with a virus that would produce a life-saving enzyme, but their bodies would not accept it. In 1980 patients with a rare but fatal blood disease were injected with a purified gene that was cloned through DNA technology. Another failure.

Genetic engineering got a legal boost in 1980. The U.S. Supreme Court said that a patent could be granted on a genetically engineered "oil-eating" bacterium. This bacterium would help clean up oil spills. The ruling encouraged companies to invent new life forms, and three important medical products were quickly developed.

- **Human interferon**—a possible solution to some cancers and viral diseases. A newly engineered bacterium produced human interferon as a by-product. This new product reduced the cost of interferon.
- **Human growth hormone**—for children whose bodies do not grow to normal height. An expensive growth hormone was previously produced from human cadavers, but by changing the genetic make-up of the single-cell bacterium *E. coli,* an affordable growth hormone could be produced.
- **Human insulin**—for the treatment of diabetes. People with diabetes used to rely on a beef- or pork-based product until 1982. Now insulin can be manufactured by genetically altered bacteria.

Advances in genetic engineering have continued, though they constantly must be <u>weighed</u> against the safety of procedures. There is clearly much more to discover.

Main Idea	1	Answer	Score
Mark the *main idea*		M	15
Mark the statement that is *too broad*		B	5
Mark the statement that is *too narrow*		N	5

a. Despite failures, genetic engineering has produced some useful products. ☐ _____

b. DNA knowledge keeps growing. ☐ _____

c. Interferon was developed as a result of genetic engineering. ☐ _____

Subject Matter   **2**   This passage is mainly about
- ☐ a. the human growth hormone.
- ☐ b. the effects of altering cells.
- ☐ c. insulin.
- ☐ d. U.S. Supreme Court rulings.   _____

Supporting Details   **3**   Interferon
- ☐ a. is a hormone.
- ☐ b. has been used in the treatment of cancer.
- ☐ c. is a disease.
- ☐ d. has been cured.   _____

Conclusion   **4**   Genetic engineering may be defined as
- ☐ a. the altering of normal cell reproduction.
- ☐ b. the production of all medicine.
- ☐ c. a procedure that holds little promise.
- ☐ d. life-saving enzymes.   _____

Clarifying Devices   **5**   In this passage, the genetically engineered medical products are presented
- ☐ a. as a process.
- ☐ b. from earliest to latest.
- ☐ c. in a simple list.
- ☐ d. in a personal narrative.   _____

Vocabulary in Context   **6**   In this passage, <u>weighed</u> means
- ☐ a. had great influence.
- ☐ b. became a burden.
- ☐ c. determined the heaviness of.
- ☐ d. considered carefully.   _____

Add your scores for questions 1–6. Enter the total here and on the graph on page 159.   Total Score   _____

51 Descended from Dinosaurs

What do ancient dinosaurs have in common with modern snakes, crocodiles, lizards, turtles, and the tuatara? They all are classified in the same formal category, the class *Reptilia*, or reptiles. Dinosaurs were only a small number of the reptiles that dominated the land, seas, and sky millions of years ago. Though dinosaurs are extinct, the reptiles of today descend from them. Reptiles are reminders of the Age of Reptiles.

Only four main groups, or orders, of reptiles live on earth today. These orders include species of alligators and crocodiles; turtles and tortoises; lizards and snakes; and a single species called the tuatara, a lizardlike animal from New Zealand. These animals at first appear to be very different, but they have many characteristics in common. All reptiles are cold-blooded—that is, they are unable to generate heat inside their own bodies. Reptiles are vertebrates, or animals with a bony skeleton that supports their bodies. They have thick, dry skin covered by scales or plates to protect them from predators and to prevent them from drying out. Finally, reptiles develop inside an egg that is protected by a leathery, waterproof shell.

Reptiles have adapted to habitats such as deserts, fresh water, oceans, swamps, plains, and cities. They also have adapted to most climates, although the tropics is their most common habitat. Reptiles come in all sizes and shapes—the gecko, which looks like a lizard, averages only 0.7 inches in length; an adult leatherback sea turtle weighs in at about 2,000 pounds. Excluding snakes, all reptiles have four limbs, usually with claws, that are used for walking, climbing, and digging. Reptiles also have well-developed respiratory and circulatory systems for breathing air through lungs and providing cells with a constant supply of oxygen. Characteristics and <u>adaptations</u> like these have enabled reptiles to survive on earth for hundreds of millions of years.

Main Idea	1		
		Answer	**Score**
	Mark the *main idea*	M	15
	Mark the statement that is *too broad*	B	5
	Mark the statement that is *too narrow*	N	5

a. Reptiles, descendants of ancient dinosaurs, have many traits in common. ☐ _____

b. Many animals are reptiles. ☐ _____

c. Reptiles are cold-blooded, meaning that they cannot generate their own body heat. ☐ _____

Subject Matter   **2**   Another good title for this passage would be

☐ a. The Small but Mighty Gecko.

☐ b. Characteristics of Vertebrates.

☐ c. Reptilia, a Class of Survivors.

☐ d. The Tropics: A Habitat for Reptiles.   _____

Supporting Details   **3**   A reptile has thick, dry skin

☐ a. because the tropical sun has damaged it.

☐ b. that always looks wet and slimy.

☐ c. that helps determine the animal's age.

☐ d. that protects the reptile and keeps it moist.   _____

Conclusion   **4**   Since a reptile cannot generate heat inside its body, it most likely

☐ a. buries itself during the summer.

☐ b. absorbs heat from its outside surroundings.

☐ c. frequently freezes to death.

☐ d. loves the cold weather.   _____

Clarifying Devices   **5**   To help the reader understand that reptiles vary greatly in size and shape, the author presents

☐ a. examples.

☐ b. scientific studies.

☐ c. vivid word pictures.

☐ d. similes and metaphors.   _____

Vocabulary in Context   **6**   In this passage, <u>adaptations</u> means

☐ a. activities.

☐ b. adjustments.

☐ c. afflictions.

☐ d. attributes.   _____

Add your scores for questions 1–6. Enter the total here and on the graph on page 160.   **Total Score**   _____

52 Seasons

Spring, summer, autumn, and winter bring changes in the weather, plant and animal life, and the length of days and nights. Seasonal changes such as these are due to three factors: the tilt of Earth's axis to one side; the rotation, or turn, of Earth on its axis every 24 hours; and the <u>revolution</u> of Earth around the sun once every year. Since Earth remains tilted in the same direction during its revolution of the sun, our distance from the sun changes, causing us to experience the changing seasons.

In summer the Northern Hemisphere, where we live, points toward the sun, bringing us closer to it and its more direct and powerful rays. Six months later, when Earth is halfway through its revolution around the sun, the Northern Hemisphere is tilted away from the sun, placing us farther from it and exposing us to the more angled, weak rays of winter. The seasons in one hemisphere are opposite those in the other hemisphere. However, one area of Earth—the equator—is always closest to the sun, so equatorial regions experience hot weather throughout the year. In contrast, the polar regions, always farthest from the sun, experience continuous frigid weather.

In the Northern Hemisphere, we observe a gradual alteration in the angle of the sun during the year. About June 21, on the summer solstice, or the first day of summer, the midday sun reaches its highest point in the sky and produces the year's maximum daylight hours. About September 22, on the autumn equinox, the midday sun is lower in the sky. Because Earth's axis is tilted neither toward nor away from the sun, equal periods of daylight and darkness result. About December 21, on the winter solstice, or the first day of winter, the midday sun is at its lowest point in the sky. This brings the year's fewest daylight hours. About March 21, on the vernal equinox, or the first day of spring, the midday sun is higher in the sky. Daytime and nighttime hours are again equal.

Main Idea 1

	Answer	Score
Mark the *main idea*	**M**	15
Mark the statement that is *too broad*	**B**	5
Mark the statement that is *too narrow*	**N**	5

a. Seasons bring many changes to Earth. ☐ _____

b. A change of seasons results from Earth's motions and the tilt of its axis. ☐ _____

c. Earth remains tilted in the same direction as it revolves around the sun. ☐ _____

Subject Matter   **2**   This passage is mainly concerned with
- ☐ a. how Earth rotates on its axis.
- ☐ b. why the various seasons occur.
- ☐ c. why each season is three months long.
- ☐ d. which parts of Earth are coldest.   _____

Supporting Details   **3**   The summer solstice results in
- ☐ a. the midday sun being at its lowest point.
- ☐ b. Earth's axis being tilted neither toward nor away from the sun.
- ☐ c. equal periods of daylight and darkness.
- ☐ d. the greatest number of daylight hours of any day during the year.   _____

Conclusion   **4**   When the Northern Hemisphere is experiencing summer, the Southern Hemisphere is experiencing
- ☐ a. winter.
- ☐ b. spring.
- ☐ c. summer.
- ☐ d. autumn.   _____

Clarifying Devices   **5**   The writer presents facts about equinoxes and solstices to explain
- ☐ a. why it is hot at the equator.
- ☐ b. the various lengths of day and night.
- ☐ c. why the midday sun is directly overhead.
- ☐ d. the date of the autumn equinox.   _____

Vocabulary in Context   **6**   In this passage, <u>revolution</u> means
- ☐ a. great change.
- ☐ b. an uprising.
- ☐ c. standing still.
- ☐ d. circling.   _____

Add your scores for questions 1–6. Enter the total here and on the graph on page 160.   **Total Score**   _____

53 Blankets of Ice

You may already know that more than a million years ago glaciers, or vast blankets of moving ice, covered nearly one-third of the earth, including northern parts of Europe, Asia, and North America. You also may know that tens of thousands of years ago the glaciers started to melt, retreating to their current positions in the Antarctic and Greenland. You might even know that glaciers also exist in all the world's great mountain regions. But do you know that glaciers cover about 6 billion square miles of the earth and store about 75 percent of the earth's fresh water?

A glacier forms in a cold climate when winter snow does not completely melt during the summer. Snow continues to accumulate and partially melt year after year. As the accumulated snow becomes heavier, the lower layer crushes under the weight and changes into ice. Over time the mass of ice thickens and moves. The ice is either pulled slowly downhill by gravity (as in the valley glaciers found in the Alps, on the Alaskan coast, and in the western United States) or forced outward in all directions by its own weight (as in the ice sheets and ice caps covering most of Greenland and Antarctica). During glaciation a glacier moves, usually about 3 feet per day. It picks up rock fragments that <u>gouge</u> and polish the land and carve out steep-sided valleys. During deglaciation a glacier recedes and often leaves large deposits of sand and gravel. This process of glaciation and deglaciation formed the Great Lakes in North America during the Ice Age.

Some scientists believe that ice ages similar to those of the past will occur, but they disagree on when this will happen. Other scientists think that global warming will occur instead, melting the glaciers and flooding many coastal areas as sea levels rise. No one knows for certain which event will occur, but neither bodes well for mankind.

Main Idea 1

	Answer	Score
Mark the *main idea*	M	15
Mark the statement that is *too broad*	B	5
Mark the statement that is *too narrow*	N	5

a. Glaciers, huge blankets of moving ice, are formed in very specific ways. ☐ _____

b. Long ago there were many glaciers. ☐ _____

c. Glaciation and deglaciation formed the Great Lakes. ☐ _____

Subject Matter   **2**   This passage is mainly about
- ☐ a. the Ice Age.
- ☐ b. valley glaciers.
- ☐ c. ice sheets and ice caps.
- ☐ d. glaciers.   _____

Supporting Details   **3**   During glaciation a glacier
- ☐ a. covers the land.
- ☐ b. retreats.
- ☐ c. melts.
- ☐ d. floods coastal areas.   _____

Conclusion   **4**   If global warming occurs instead of another ice age,
- ☐ a. vast blankets of ice will cover the earth.
- ☐ b. glaciers in the Antarctic will increase in size.
- ☐ c. plant and animal life in many areas will be destroyed.
- ☐ d. a winter's snow may not completely melt during the following summer.   _____

Clarifying Devices   **5**   To help the reader understand how a glacier forms, the author
- ☐ a. gives a step-by-step explanation.
- ☐ b. presents a detailed example.
- ☐ c. makes a strong argument.
- ☐ d. cites careful measurements.   _____

Vocabulary in Context   **6**   In this passage, <u>gouge</u> means
- ☐ a. trick or cheat.
- ☐ b. cut holes into.
- ☐ c. smooth out.
- ☐ d. raise the surface of.   _____

Add your scores for questions 1–6. Enter the total here and on the graph on page 160.   Total Score   _____

54 In or out of the Water?

Frogs and toads, salamanders and newts, and the little-known caecilian are amphibians, a word derived from the Greek *amphibios,* meaning "double life." The name is a good one to describe these animals that live part of their lives in water and part on land.

Structurally the groups of amphibians are very different. Frogs and toads, for example, are tailless. They have short, thick bodies, two short forelegs, and two long powerful hind legs. Salamanders and newts have long tails, lizard-shaped bodies, and two pairs of equal-sized limbs. Caecilians may have short pointed tails.

Although amphibians are structurally diverse, they have many similar characteristics. All amphibians are vertebrates, or animals with backbones that give the body shape and provide for movement. Amphibians have a circulatory system consisting of blood vessels and a three-chambered heart that moves the blood to and from all parts of the body. Amphibians also possess a well-developed nervous system that lets them receive and react to messages from their surroundings. Amphibians are cold-blooded, meaning that their body temperature changes with their surroundings. Amphibians also have a thin moist skin with no surface scales, hair, or feathers.

Reproduction usually occurs in water, where female amphibians lay eggs with a jelly coating but no protective shell. Male amphibians fertilize the eggs by spreading sperm directly over them in the water. A characteristic of most amphibians is the metamorphosis, or series of body changes, that they undergo. After hatching from eggs, most young amphibians continue to live in water, taking in oxygen from the water as it flows over their gills. As amphibians change into adults, however, most develop lungs and reside on land at least part of the time. Those adult amphibians that live on land can also <u>respire</u> through their skin if they return to the water.

Main Idea 1	Answer	Score
Mark the *main idea*	M	15
Mark the statement that is *too broad*	B	5
Mark the statement that is *too narrow*	N	5

a. Amphibians have thin moist skins with no surface scales, hair, or feathers. ☐ _____

b. Amphibians are a type of animal. ☐ _____

c. Amphibians are structurally diverse but have a number of similar characteristics. ☐ _____

Score 15 points for each correct answer.   Score

Subject Matter   **2**   This passage focuses primarily on
- ☐ a. caecilians.
- ☐ b. frogs and toads.
- ☐ c. salamanders and newts.
- ☐ d. qualities of amphibians.   _____

Supporting Details   **3**   During metamorphosis, most amphibians
- ☐ a. develop backbones.
- ☐ b. form a circulatory system.
- ☐ c. replace gills with lungs.
- ☐ d. reproduce by laying eggs with a jelly coating.   _____

Conclusion   **4**   The last sentence of this passage suggests that amphibians are
- ☐ a. unable to stand change.
- ☐ b. adaptable.
- ☐ c. large.
- ☐ d. noisy at certain times in their lives.   _____

Clarifying Devices   **5**   The word *although* at the beginning of the third paragraph signals
- ☐ a. a contrast.
- ☐ b. a similarity.
- ☐ c. an additional piece of information.
- ☐ d. a choice.   _____

Vocabulary in Context   **6**   The word <u>respire</u> means to
- ☐ a. grow.
- ☐ b. reproduce.
- ☐ c. swim.
- ☐ d. breathe.   _____

Add your scores for questions 1–6. Enter the total here and on the graph on page 160.   Total Score   _____

55 Peering into the Sky

Astronomy is the study of the planets, stars, and other objects in space. About 400 years ago, the Dutch lensmaker Hans Lippershey held a glass lens at arm's length and looked at it through another lens held in front of his eye. He discovered that the two lenses magnified distant objects and made them brighter. This discovery led to the first optical telescope. An optical telescope uses visible light rays to produce images of distant objects. Optical telescopes with lenses are called refracting telescopes. As light passes through air and then through the lenses of a refracting telescope, the light refracts, or bends. These bent light rays create a problem in that they cause tiny "rainbows" to appear around the produced images. Another problem is that over time heavy lenses sag, which further <u>distorts</u> images created by them.

In 1668 Isaac Newton developed an optical telescope with mirrors, called a reflecting telescope. In a reflecting telescope, light rays coming from a distant object reflect off mirrors and create a focused image of the object. Because the image is focused, the reflecting telescope is the main optical telescope used by astronomers. Visible light, however, is only one way in which astronomers learn about space. Objects in space also send invisible rays toward Earth. Different types of telescopes detect x-rays and other invisible rays such as radio, infrared, ultraviolet, and gamma rays.

A drawback of telescopes based on Earth is that rays from space pass through Earth's atmosphere before they reach the telescopes. Smog, clouds, winds, and precipitation in Earth's atmosphere filter out and refract some of these rays. The images and signals that reach telescopes on Earth often appear shifting and blurry. To obtain more accurate images, scientists employ rockets, satellites, and other spacecraft to carry telescopes high above Earth's atmosphere.

Main Idea 1

	Answer	Score
Mark the *main idea*	M	15
Mark the statement that is *too broad*	B	5
Mark the statement that is *too narrow*	N	5

a. There are several types of telescopes. ☐ _____

b. Light bends in a refracting telescope. ☐ _____

c. Optical and other types of telescopes have both advantages and disadvantages. ☐ _____

Score 15 points for each correct answer.   **Score**

Subject Matter   **2**   This passage is mainly about
- ☐ a. rays sent by objects in space toward Earth.
- ☐ b. different types of telescopes.
- ☐ c. "rainbows" produced by refracted light rays.
- ☐ d. differences between visible light rays and invisible rays.

_____

Supporting Details   **3**   Reflecting telescopes use
- ☐ a. satellites.
- ☐ b. radio waves.
- ☐ c. x-rays.
- ☐ d. mirrors.

_____

Conclusion   **4**   Earth-orbiting telescopes provide more accurate information than earthbound telescopes because
- ☐ a. rays from space are not distorted in Earth's atmosphere.
- ☐ b. earth-orbiting telescopes are more powerful.
- ☐ c. invisible rays are stronger than visible rays.
- ☐ d. earth-orbiting telescopes contain better mirrors.

_____

Clarifying Devices   **5**   In the first paragraph, "rainbows" is put in quotation marks to show that
- ☐ a. these are the exact words of a speaker.
- ☐ b. this is an unusual spelling of a word.
- ☐ c. the items being described aren't really rainbows.
- ☐ d. the images show up only after a storm.

_____

Vocabulary in Context   **6**   In this passage, <u>distorts</u> means to make
- ☐ a. unclear.
- ☐ b. clear.
- ☐ c. larger.
- ☐ d. smaller.

_____

Add your scores for questions 1–6. Enter the total here and on the graph on page 160.   **Total Score**   _____

56 The Earth's Blankets

You may watch those fluffy white formations floating across the sky for fun, but scientists watch them in hopes of accurately forecasting and eventually controlling or modifying the weather. Clouds are one visible element of a day's weather. They are formed when the sun heats the earth, which then radiates thermal energy to the air in its atmosphere. Since warm air is less dense than cool air, the heated air creates "thermal updrafts" that rise up and away from the earth. The temperature in the atmosphere decreases with <u>altitude</u>. As the warm air rises, it cools, and the water vapor in it condenses into tiny droplets of water or particles of ice, depending on the altitude. These liquid or ice particles are visible as a cloud.

Clouds affect the earth's weather and climate. Acting as sort of a blanket between the sun and the earth, they prevent sunlight from reaching and warming the earth and block the amount of infrared radiation, or radiating heat, escaping from the earth into outer space. Thus, weather observers know that a cloudy day will be cooler than a clear day and that a cloudy night will be warmer than a clear night.

Scientists have divided clouds into three main classes—cirrus, cumulus, and stratus. *Cirrus,* a Latin word meaning "curl," describes white wispy clouds stretching across the sky at high altitudes. *Cumulus,* a Latin word meaning "heap," characterizes piles of flat-based cottonlike clouds at low altitudes. *Stratus,* derived from a Latin word meaning "spread out," identifies layers of flat gray clouds spreading across the sky at low altitudes. Scientists use these three classes to specify the numerous combinations of clouds that exist. Masses of gray and white clouds rolling across the sky are stratocumulus. The Latin word *nimbus,* meaning "rain cloud," is added to a precipitating cloud. Cumulonimbus describes cumulus clouds producing thunderstorms.

Main Idea 1

	Answer	Score
Mark the *main idea*	M	15
Mark the statement that is *too broad*	B	5
Mark the statement that is *too narrow*	N	5

a. Cloudy days are cooler than sunny ones. ☐ _____

b. Clouds are fluffy white formations floating across the sky. ☐ _____

c. Clouds, which affect the earth's weather, come in three main classes. ☐ _____

Score 15 points for each correct answer.　　　　**Score**

Subject Matter 　**2**　This passage is mainly about
　　　　　　　　　☐ a. the importance and classification of clouds.
　　　　　　　　　☐ b. how thermal updrafts produce weather.
　　　　　　　　　☐ c. precipitation and why it occurs.
　　　　　　　　　☐ d. why condensation occurs in the atmosphere.　　_____

Supporting　　　**3**　Clouds are
Details　　　　　☐ a. a weather forecaster's nightmare.
　　　　　　　　　☐ b. infrared radiation escaping the atmosphere.
　　　　　　　　　☐ c. visible liquid or ice particles in the air.
　　　　　　　　　☐ d. a source of thermal energy.　　_____

Conclusion　　　**4**　We can conclude that a cloudy night will be
　　　　　　　　　warmer than a clear night because
　　　　　　　　　☐ a. clouds trap the earth's heat in the area
　　　　　　　　　　　between the ground and the clouds.
　　　　　　　　　☐ b. infrared radiation escapes into outer space.
　　　　　　　　　☐ c. there will be few or no stars visible.
　　　　　　　　　☐ d. clouds prevent much of the sun's heat from
　　　　　　　　　　　reaching the earth.　　_____

Clarifying　　　**5**　The Latin definitions in the third paragraph are
Devices　　　　　intended to help you
　　　　　　　　　☐ a. spell the names of clouds correctly.
　　　　　　　　　☐ b. visualize the various types of clouds.
　　　　　　　　　☐ c. see that there are only three types of clouds.
　　　　　　　　　☐ d. memorize the names of clouds.　　_____

Vocabulary　　　**6**　<u>Altitude</u> means
in Context　　　　☐ a. width.
　　　　　　　　　☐ b. height.
　　　　　　　　　☐ c. depth.
　　　　　　　　　☐ d. circumference.　　_____

Add your scores for questions 1–6. Enter the total here　　**Total**
and on the graph on page 160.　　**Score**　　_____

57 To Soar Like a Bird

Designs are underway for a double-decker superjet capable of transporting up to 1,000 passengers and containing such convenience facilities as a health club, a medical treatment center, shops, sleeping compartments, and elevators. How is it possible for such a monstrous airliner to take flight, let alone stay airborne? The idea becomes believable when you understand the relationship between moving fluids and pressure. Bernoulli's law states that as a fluid, such as a gas or a liquid, travels faster, the pressure exerted by the fluid decreases. This explains the lift, or upward force, that allows airplanes to fly even though they are heavier than air, which is a gas.

Lift is created by airfoils, or wings, that are rounded in the front and narrowed in the back. In the middle, the wings are thick, and their surface is more rounded on the upper side than the lower side. The curved upper surface provides a greater distance for air to flow across than does the flatter lower surface. The greater distance across the wing's upper surface causes the air above the wing to flow faster than the air beneath. The air pressure of the slower-flowing air beneath the wing is greater than that of the faster-flowing air above it. The greater air pressure beneath the wing exerts an upward force, and lift results. The greater an airplane's thrust, or forward-moving force, the faster the airplane moves and the greater the lift. When the lift becomes greater than the weight of the plane, the airplane overcomes gravity and rises. In level flight, the lift force on an airplane's wings is equal to the weight of the airplane.

Airplane manufacturers may be capable of designing superjets that can attain and maintain lift. Have they contemplated, though, how to efficiently deplane 1,000 impatient passengers and <u>process</u> them through a crowded airport? Even worse, have they anticipated the lines of expectant passengers waiting at the baggage claim?

Main Idea	1	Answer	Score
Mark the *main idea*		M	15
Mark the statement that is *too broad*		B	5
Mark the statement that is *too narrow*		N	5

a. There are forces that allow planes to fly even though they are heavier than air. ☐ _____

b. Flight is a complicated process. ☐ _____

c. Airfoils are rounded in the front, curved in the middle, and narrowed in the back. ☐ _____

Score 15 points for each correct answer.　　　　**Score**

Subject Matter　**2**　Another good title for this passage would be
　　　　　　☐ a. Bernoulli and His Law.
　　　　　　☐ b. Getting a Lift from Moving Air.
　　　　　　☐ c. The Friendly Skies Have It All.
　　　　　　☐ d. Flying Across Continents.　　　_____

Supporting　　**3**　To understand flight, you must understand
Details　　　　the relationship between
　　　　　　☐ a. moving fluids and pressure.
　　　　　　☐ b. air and force.
　　　　　　☐ c. speed and gravity.
　　　　　　☐ d. surfaces and tension.　　　_____

Conclusion　　**4**　Bernoulli's law was probably established
　　　　　　☐ a. before the Wright brothers flew in 1903.
　　　　　　☐ b. just after the Wright brothers flew.
　　　　　　☐ c. just before the flight of the first passenger jet
　　　　　　　　in 1958.
　　　　　　☐ d. just after the flight of the first passenger jet.　_____

Clarifying　　**5**　To make the point that a superjet in the skies may
Devices　　　　not be so super on the ground, the author
　　　　　　☐ a. presents the conveniences of the superjet.
　　　　　　☐ b. explains the purpose of airfoils.
　　　　　　☐ c. discusses the superjet's effects on airports.
　　　　　　☐ d. defines lift in terms of air and pressure.　　_____

Vocabulary　　**6**　In this passage, <u>process</u> means
in Context　　　☐ a. advance in an orderly manner.
　　　　　　☐ b. a gradual change.
　　　　　　☐ c. a natural phenomenon.
　　　　　　☐ d. expect unreasonable delays.　　　_____

Add your scores for questions 1–6. Enter the total here　**Total**
and on the graph on page 160.　　　　　**Score**　_____

58 Physical, Chemical, or Nuclear?

You know matter is anything that has mass and occupies space. You may not know that matter contains energy that can be converted from one form to another (for example, from solar energy to electric energy) and that matter gains or releases energy as it changes form. These transformations occur in physical, chemical, and nuclear changes.

A physical change is an alteration in the form of matter but not in its <u>composition</u>. A change of state, such as from a solid to a liquid or a gas, is a physical change. For example, water forms ice in its solid state and steam in its gaseous state, but the composition of the particles in each state remains the same—water molecules. During a physical change, matter *sometimes gains or releases energy,* usually as heat.

In a chemical change, one type of matter is converted into another. For example, when iron comes into contact with oxygen and water in air, the iron changes into rust. The atoms of the iron and oxygen and of the water molecules rearrange themselves and produce a new matter—rust. The composition of rust is chemically different from the original substances. During a chemical change, matter *always gains or releases energy.*

In a nuclear change, the nucleus of an element's atom is altered, thus producing a different element. In one type of nuclear change, fission, a single large nucleus splits into smaller nuclei. For example, the nucleus of a uranium atom may divide into two nuclei—a nucleus of the element barium and a nucleus of the element krypton. During a nuclear change, matter *always releases energy*—and it releases a considerable amount. A quantity of uranium about the size of a golf ball produces as much energy as one million kilograms of coal. Scientists utilize these qualities of matter to improve existing energy sources and to search for new energy sources to provide power for commonly used items.

Main Idea	1	Answer	Score
	Mark the *main idea*	M	15
	Mark the statement that is *too broad*	B	5
	Mark the statement that is *too narrow*	N	5

    a. During a nuclear change, matter always releases energy. ☐ _____

    b. Changes to matter occur during many processes. ☐ _____

    c. Matter is transformed during physical, chemical, and nuclear changes. ☐ _____

Score 15 points for each correct answer.   **Score**

Subject Matter   **2**   Another good title for this passage would be
    ☐ a. Matter: Create Energy by Changing It.
    ☐ b. Steam: It's Such a Gas.
    ☐ c. Changes of State: It's Physical.
    ☐ d. Fission: We're Just Splitting Atoms.   _____

Supporting   **3**   In a chemical change, the original matter is
Details   altered so that the new substance that is formed is
    ☐ a. of the same composition as the original.
    ☐ b. only a change of state.
    ☐ c. chemically different from the original.
    ☐ d. split into two or more nuclei.   _____

Conclusion   **4**   You can conclude from this passage that scientists
searching for improved energy sources are most
likely to explore
    ☐ a. composition changes.
    ☐ b. nuclear changes.
    ☐ c. physical changes.
    ☐ d. chemical changes.   _____

Clarifying   **5**   To help the reader compare what happens to
Devices   energy in the three types of changes, the writer
    ☐ a. italicizes key phrases.
    ☐ b. underlines key terms.
    ☐ c. states scientific facts.
    ☐ d. quantifies amounts.   _____

Vocabulary   **6**   In this passage, <u>composition</u> refers to
in Context
    ☐ a. an essay.
    ☐ b. a piece of written music.
    ☐ c. the makeup of a substance.
    ☐ d. an arrangement.   _____

Add your scores for questions 1–6. Enter the total here   **Total**
and on the graph on page 160.   **Score**   _____

59 Falling from the Skies

Technological advancements in the 20th century have made people healthier and more comfortable than ever before. Automobiles, telephones, and computers are everyday conveniences for many people. Oil-refining techniques and nuclear energy provide power for vehicles and communities. Drug therapies and medical technology improve and prolong life. Fertilizers and pesticides produce more fertile harvests. Plastics strengthen materials and fabrics. Satellites and shuttles explore distant regions in space. The <u>downside</u> to these developments, however, lies in how they affect the earth's environment.

The production processes for many of these advances require the burning of fossil fuels such as coal and oil. The combustion of these resources releases sulfur dioxide and nitrogen oxide gases, which react with oxygen and water in the atmosphere. The result is sulfuric and nitric acids that are carried to earth with rain, hail, and snow. This acid rain, or acid precipitation, falls on buildings and mountains, seeps into soil, and mixes into groundwater as well as into the waters of oceans, lakes, and rivers. Too much acid kills fish and other water-dwelling organisms. It breaks down soil nutrients and prevents plant growth. It even corrodes metals and dissolves the limestone and concrete of buildings and other structures.

Scientists fear that acid rain will destroy life's basic necessities—air, water, food, and shelter. We must take action to stop acid rain now! Let's start by burning only low-sulfur oil and coal and installing scrubbers in smokestacks to reduce oxides released into the air, and let's equip trucks with pollution-control devices to remove sulfur gases from exhaust. Big business and government argue that such measures are too expensive, but delaying action will be costly in other ways for future generations.

Main Idea	1		Answer	Score
	Mark the *main idea*		M	15
	Mark the statement that is *too broad*		B	5
	Mark the statement that is *too narrow*		N	5

a. Acid rain, a result of technological development, is destroying many parts of our environment. ☐ _____

b. Too much acid kills fish and other water-dwelling organisms. ☐ _____

c. Acid rain is very destructive. ☐

Score 15 points for each correct answer.   **Score**

Subject Matter   **2**   The passage focuses mainly on
                              ☐ a. technological development in the future.
                              ☐ b. the long-term effects of acid rain.
                              ☐ c. how to develop low-nitrogen fertilizers.
                              ☐ d. big business and government decisions.   _____

Supporting   **3**   Sulfuric acid forms as a result of
Details   ☐ a. fossil fuels such as coal releasing energy.
                          ☐ b. low-sulfur oil and coal being installed in
                                smokestacks.
                          ☐ c. rain, hail, and snow falling.
                          ☐ d. sulfur dioxide combining with water and
                                oxygen.   _____

Conclusion   **4**   The writer of this passage
                          ☐ a. thinks it costs too much to get rid of acid rain.
                          ☐ b. blames ordinary citizens for acid rain.
                          ☐ c. believes acid rain has no effect on children.
                          ☐ d. has strong feelings about acid rain.   _____

Clarifying   **5**   The writer discusses technological advances to
Devices   help the reader understand that such developments
                          ☐ a. have had both good and bad results.
                          ☐ b. make life easier for people.
                          ☐ c. have produced much wealth for big business.
                          ☐ d. are good for the earth's atmosphere.   _____

Vocabulary   **6**   In this passage, <u>downside</u> means
in Context   ☐ a. underneath part.
                          ☐ b. a lowering of gears.
                          ☐ c. a heavy rain.
                          ☐ d. bad part.   _____

Add your scores for questions 1–6. Enter the total here   **Total**
and on the graph on page 160.   **Score**   _____

60 Achieving Cardiovascular Fitness

Heart attacks, strokes, and other cardiovascular diseases are the leading cause of death in the developed world. These diseases include disorders of the blood vessels that pump and carry blood throughout the body. In a disorder called *atherosclerosis,* for instance, the aorta or other major blood vessels become clogged with fatty deposits of cholesterol. As cholesterol builds up, the walls of the vessels harden and thicken. The narrowed passages in the vessels slow the flow of blood cells—and the oxygen they carry—to the brain and to the heart and other muscles. When the heart is deprived of oxygen-rich blood, a heart attack occurs. If oxygen-rich blood doesn't reach the brain, a stroke results. Such cardiovascular diseases are likely in people who are overweight or smoke cigarettes. Other risk factors include high blood pressure, heart disease, and high cholesterol. Regular exercise can help a person reduce these risk factors.

Aerobic exercise, such as jogging, walking, skating, and swimming, helps people to become cardiovascularly fit. An aerobic workout must be vigorous so that the heart, lungs, blood vessels, and skeletal muscles constantly use energy. During aerobic activities, the muscle cells undergo aerobic metabolism. In this process, oxygen combines with a fuel source (fats or carbohydrates) to release energy and produce carbon dioxide and water. The muscle cells use the energy to <u>contract</u>, which creates a force that produces movement. The aerobic reaction only occurs if the circulatory and pulmonary systems provide a constant supply of oxygen and fuel to the muscle cells and remove carbon dioxide from them. Most people can achieve cardiovascular fitness by raising their heart and breathing rates for 25 to 30 minutes about every other day. Those people will have the energy to do easily all the things they want to do.

Main Idea	1	Answer	Score
	Mark the *main idea*	M	15
	Mark the statement that is *too broad*	B	5
	Mark the statement that is *too narrow*	N	5

a. Cardiovascular diseases cause many deaths. ☐ _____

b. Cardiovascular diseases are dangerous, but aerobic exercise can prevent them. ☐ _____

c. Atherosclerosis causes hardening and thickening of major blood vessels. ☐ _____

Subject Matter   **2**   Another good title for this passage would be
- ☐ a. Overweight with High Blood Pressure.
- ☐ b. Kinds of Cardiovascular Diseases.
- ☐ c. Fats and Carbohydrates.
- ☐ d. Avoiding Cardiovascular Diseases.   _____

Supporting Details   **3**   A person will gain from aerobic exercise if he or she
- ☐ a. raises and maintains the heart and breathing rates on a regular basis.
- ☐ b. monitors the heart rate while exercising.
- ☐ c. eats fats and carbohydrates for energy.
- ☐ d. takes a break after every 10 minutes of vigorous exercise.   _____

Conclusion   **4**   We can conclude that the more risk factors a person has for cardiovascular disease, the
- ☐ a. fewer the chances of getting the disease.
- ☐ b. greater the chances of getting the disease.
- ☐ c. more likely it is that the person smokes.
- ☐ d. less likely it is that the person is overweight.   _____

Clarifying Devices   **5**   The sentence "if oxygen-rich blood doesn't reach the brain, a stroke results" is an example of
- ☐ a. persuasion.
- ☐ b. narration.
- ☐ c. definition.
- ☐ d. cause and effect.   _____

Vocabulary in Context   **6**   In this passage, <u>contract</u> means
- ☐ a. an agreement between two people.
- ☐ b. to form words like _don't_ and _can't_.
- ☐ c. to tighten or make shorter.
- ☐ d. to get or bring on oneself.   _____

Add your scores for questions 1–6. Enter the total here and on the graph on page 160.   **Total Score**   _____

61 Earth Moved

Earthquakes can happen anywhere on Earth, but these natural geological events are more common in some areas than in others. The lithosphere—a 60-mile thickness of the earth's crust and the uppermost layer of its mantle—is separated into huge slabs called tectonic plates. These plates are constantly colliding, and the rock within them accumulates great stresses after many years of continuous grinding. Eventually the stresses exceed the strength of the rock, causing it to suddenly shift position and explosively discharge seismic waves of energy.

The seismic waves travel outward from the focus, or point of origin inside the lithosphere, and <u>span</u> the earth at speeds of about 15,000 miles per hour. However, only waves in the vicinity of the earthquake's epicenter, the point on the earth's surface directly above the focus, will be strong enough to cause damage. The fastest waves to arrive at the epicenter are the primary, or P, waves that push and pull as they travel. P waves are not very big, and they often can be heard but not felt. The secondary, or S, waves are the next to arrive. S waves produce a side-to-side shaking as they travel, thus causing people and things near the epicenter to shake from side to side. The slowest waves, surface waves, produce a rolling movement. Surface waves may be violent enough to reduce entire cities to rubble, to kill or injure thousands of people, and to create faults, or cracks, deep in the rock of the earth's surface.

Scientists often know where an earthquake will occur, but they cannot accurately predict its timing. Earthquake preparation—that is, the education of people so they know what to do during an earthquake and the construction of earthquake-resistant buildings, bridges, and roads—may minimize an earthquake's aftereffects.

Main Idea 1		Answer	Score
Mark the *main idea*		M	15
Mark the statement that is *too broad*		B	5
Mark the statement that is *too narrow*		N	5

a. Only waves near an earthquake's epicenter are likely to cause damage. ☐ _____

b. Earthquakes are natural events that originate from deep within the earth. ☐ _____

c. Earthquakes occur in many places on the earth. ☐ _____

Subject Matter   **2**   The main purpose of this passage is to
☐ a. define epicenters.
☐ b. explain the formation of faults.
☐ c. describe types of seismic waves.
☐ d. tell what happens in an earthquake.   _____

Supporting Details   **3**   An epicenter is
☐ a. the point on the earth's surface just above an earthquake's point of origin.
☐ b. a large slab of the earth's crust.
☐ c. the exact point where an earthquake begins.
☐ d. a huge rolling wave of energy.   _____

Conclusion   **4**   The most destructive waves produced by a quake are
☐ a. seismic waves.
☐ b. surface waves.
☐ c. S waves.
☐ d. P waves.   _____

Clarifying Devices   **5**   Which of these terms does the writer *not* define?
☐ a. mantle
☐ b. lithosphere
☐ c. focus
☐ d. earthquake preparation   _____

Vocabulary in Context   **6**   In this passage, <u>span</u> means
☐ a. the length of a bridge.
☐ b. to extend across.
☐ c. an individual's lifetime.
☐ d. to build a support over.   _____

Add your scores for questions 1–6. Enter the total here and on the graph on page 160.   **Total Score**   _____

62 An Intense Beam of Light

Our society uses lasers in many areas of science, medicine, communications, industry, and the military. We also utilize lasers in such commonplace devices as bar code scanners, radar speed-detectors, CD and videodisk players, and laser pointers. Laser technology is relatively new, but a <u>theoretical</u> laser was proposed by Albert Einstein in 1917. It wasn't until 1960, however, that technology allowed for construction of the first laser. That laser was made of a solid ruby medium (a substance that transmits energy) that produced an intense beam of pure red light. Lasers today are made of a variety of materials, each of which emits an intense beam of light having one pure color.

The word *laser*—an acronym for **l**ight **a**mplification by **s**timulated **e**mission of **r**adiation—describes how the device works. A laser has three main parts: an energy source, such as intense ordinary light; a medium of ions, molecules, or atoms; and a mirror at either end of the medium—one mirror to reflect the light that strikes it and one to output part of the light. The atoms of the medium exist at low- and high-energy levels. When the energy source activates, the low-energy atoms absorb the energy and become excited to a higher level. Some of the excited atoms spontaneously radiate light waves in random directions and then return to their low-energy level. Many of the light waves become trapped between the mirrors, staying within the medium and striking high-energy atoms. The high-energy atoms become stimulated and emit light of the same wavelength as the light wave that stimulated them. The emitted light amplifies the passing light wave. By repeatedly activating the energy source, the cycle continues, making the light wave bigger and stronger. Eventually some of the wave bursts through the output mirror as a laser beam—a tremendously powerful radiating light wave.

Main Idea	1	Answer	Score
	Mark the *main idea*	M	15
	Mark the statement that is *too broad*	B	5
	Mark the statement that is *too narrow*	N	5

		Answer	Score
a.	Our society uses lasers in many different areas.	☐	_____
b.	The first laser produced an intense beam of pure red light.	☐	_____
c.	*Laser* is an acronym for the words that describe how a laser works.	☐	_____

Subject Matter   **2**   The purpose of this passage is to
- [ ] a. identify the uses of lasers in our society.
- [ ] b. describe the history of lasers.
- [ ] c. explain how lasers work.
- [ ] d. compare low-energy atoms with high-energy atoms.

_____

Supporting Details   **3**   The following is not part of today's lasers:
- [ ] a. an energy source.
- [ ] b. a ruby.
- [ ] c. a medium of ions or molecules.
- [ ] d. a pair of mirrors.

_____

Conclusion   **4**   We can conclude that the light wave reflects back and forth within the laser until
- [ ] a. the low-energy atoms become excited.
- [ ] b. spontaneous light radiation occurs.
- [ ] c. the medium becomes weak.
- [ ] d. the wave has enough energy to escape.

_____

Clarifying Devices   **5**   To demonstrate what an acronym is, the writer
- [ ] a. uses boldface type for the first letters of words.
- [ ] b. underlines the word.
- [ ] c. compares it to an abbreviation.
- [ ] d. tells how many parts there are.

_____

Vocabulary in Context   **6**   Theoretical means
- [ ] a. very small.
- [ ] b. based on theory, not fact.
- [ ] c. very large.
- [ ] d. capable of causing accidents.

_____

Add your scores for questions 1–6. Enter the total here and on the graph on page 160.   **Total Score**

_____

63 Is It Real, or Is It . . . ?

You pause in your descent from the mountaintop and walk out onto a rocky overhang. With one more step, you're standing at the edge. You cautiously look down, careful not to lose your balance. You're taken aback by the startling landscape. Nowhere else in the solar system have you seen such a spectacular view—a mix of cliffs and plateaus painted in vivid hues of yellow-browns and dark reddish-purples. You're still in awe as you turn away, eager to explore Mars's Mariner Valley below.

Although the passage above reads like science fiction, it describes what you could experience if you were to visit a virtual-reality lab. Virtual reality engages the user in a computer-generated environment that simulates, or imitates, reality. The user wears special equipment, often in the form of a head-mounted-display (HMD) such as goggles or a headset. Inside the HMD are two tiny video screens, one in front of each eye. The computer sends a slightly different image onto each screen, thus creating an illusion of depth. This false <u>perception</u> gives the user the feeling of being in the midst of a three-dimensional world. Sensors in the HMD track the user's head movements and inform the computer to update the scene on the video screens in "real time" with each movement. Some virtual reality systems may also include sensors in gloves or bodysuits that let the user interact more fully with the virtual environment.

You may be familiar with virtual reality from the "realistic" video games that totally immerse players in a three-dimensional interactive world. Scientists, however, continue to explore virtual reality as a learning tool. Applications of this science include such areas as space exploration, medicine, pilot training, architecture, chemistry, biotechnology, engineering—and even driver's education.

Main Idea	1	Answer	Score
	Mark the *main idea*	M	15
	Mark the statement that is *too broad*	B	5
	Mark the statement that is *too narrow*	N	5

a. Virtual reality is a computer-generated environment that simulates reality. ☐ _____

b. The mind can be tricked through various computer devices. ☐ _____

c. Some video games use virtual reality. ☐ _____

Score 15 points for each correct answer.　　　　**Score**

Subject Matter　**2**　This passage is concerned with
☐ a. why people like science fiction.
☐ b. the Mariner Valley of Mars.
☐ c. how virtual reality works.
☐ d. applications of science technology.　　　____

Supporting Details　**3**　The HMD contains two video screens to
☐ a. track the user's movements.
☐ b. simulate a game.
☐ c. fill the space in front of the eyes.
☐ d. create an illusion of depth.　　　____

Conclusion　**4**　The HMD, data gloves, and bodysuit create the illusion that the user is
☐ a. an active member of a real environment.
☐ b. playing a computer game.
☐ c. watching a film.
☐ d. a bit confused by the world.　　　____

Clarifying Devices　**5**　The author italicized the first paragraph to
☐ a. give readers something different to look at.
☐ b. present details about virtual reality.
☐ c. discuss HMD tracking systems.
☐ d. signal a different type of writing.　　　____

Vocabulary in Context　**6**　In this passage, perception means
☐ a. heat or electricity.
☐ b. observation or understanding.
☐ c. the act of clarifying something.
☐ d. the ability to make a sound conclusion.　　　____

Add your scores for questions 1–6. Enter the total here and on the graph on page 160.　　　**Total Score**　____

64 Weathering

Mountains, plains, and coastlines seem solid and immovable beneath our feet, but in reality the earth around us is in a state of constant change. It's changing along shores as powerful waves pound into the rock of a cliff. It's changing on windy days as airborne particles gouge into the surface of anything in their path. It's changing both on sweltering sunny days and on frigid snowy days. The <u>disintegration</u> of rock that takes place at or near the surface of the earth is called weathering.

Physical weathering occurs when a force is applied to rock, causing it to disintegrate into its basic components. The principal sources of physical weathering are temperature change, which expands and contracts rock particles and thus breaks rock apart; frost action, which condenses water vapor in cooling air to form water that seeps into cracks in rock; and organic activity, which occurs when plants and other organisms grow and burrow into cracks in rock, causing the rock to crumble over time.

Chemical weathering occurs when substances such as water, sulfuric acid, and plant acids cause changes in the mineral composition or chemical makeup of rock. Many minerals in rocks react chemically with substances in the damp atmosphere. Limestone, for example, is weathered by the carbon dioxide in rainwater, which slowly eats away the rock.

While weathering breaks down rocks to form loose material or rock minerals, erosion removes the material and rock minerals from their original location and transports them to other locations. These combined forces of weathering and erosion have been shaping the familiar landscapes of the earth for millions of years.

Main Idea	1	Answer	Score
	Mark the *main idea*	M	15
	Mark the statement that is *too broad*	B	5
	Mark the statement that is *too narrow*	N	5

a. The earth around us is in a state of constant change. ☐ _____

b. Chemical weathering results from changes in the chemical makeup of rock. ☐ _____

c. Weathering is an ongoing process caused by physical and chemical processes. ☐ _____

Subject Matter   **2**   Another good title for this passage would be
- ☐ a. Weather Patterns and Climate.
- ☐ b. The Changing Face of the Earth.
- ☐ c. Our Eroding Mountains.
- ☐ d. Rocks, Minerals, and Fragments.

          _____

Supporting Details   **3**   Physical weathering may be caused by all of the following *except*
- ☐ a. frost action.
- ☐ b. plant acids.
- ☐ c. temperature change.
- ☐ d. organic activity.

          _____

Conclusion   **4**   A good example of weathering is
- ☐ a. heavy ice breaking chunks off a rock face.
- ☐ b. water removing sand from a beach and putting it elsewhere.
- ☐ c. wind breaking the windows in a building.
- ☐ d. heavy rain causing rivers to flood.

          _____

Clarifying Devices   **5**   The writer introduces the concept of weathering by
- ☐ a. presenting examples that we might be familiar with.
- ☐ b. describing mountains, plains, and coasts.
- ☐ c. explaining how wind speeds constantly change.
- ☐ d. defining physical and chemical processes.

          _____

Vocabulary in Context   **6**   In this passage, <u>disintegration</u> means
- ☐ a. breaking into parts.
- ☐ b. uniting into a whole.
- ☐ c. creation of newer, larger substances.
- ☐ d. restoration to a previous condition.

          _____

Add your scores for questions 1–6. Enter the total here and on the graph on page 160.   Total Score   _____

65 Bacteria Killers

In 1928 Scottish scientist Alexander Fleming was searching for methods of treating infections. He found that a mold of the genus *Penicillium* had accidentally contaminated a culture of bacteria and stopped its growth. Fleming named the mold's antibacterial substance penicillin. He recognized the therapeutic potential of his discovery, but his penicillin produced inconsistent results as a treatment against infections. Fleming's penicillin proved to be impure and weak. It was not until 1941 that two scientists, Howard Florey and Ernst Chain, came up with a purer, more stable penicillin. During World War II, methods were developed to mass produce the drug so that it could fight infections in injured Allied troops. By the end of the war, penicillin was made available to the general public. Penicillin soon became the miracle drug of the 20th century.

Penicillin is an antibiotic, or a chemical produced by living organisms—usually bacteria or molds—that retard or stop the growth of bacteria. Antibiotics weaken the cell walls of reproducing bacteria, causing the new cells to grow abnormally. After several days of treatment with antibiotics, few bacterial cells survive. Along with penicillin, other widely used antibiotics are ampicillin and streptomycin. These antibiotics are used to fight infectious diseases, such as meningitis, pneumonia, strep throat, and staph infections.

In recent years, antibiotics have become less effective. One reason may be that they have been used too frequently. Scientists have discovered that bacteria can develop a <u>resistance</u> to antibiotics by forming genetic mutations. These genetic changes let the mutants survive and reproduce. While scientists continue to search for new sources of antibiotics, they caution doctors not to overprescribe these drugs.

Main Idea	1	Answer	Score
	Mark the *main idea*	M	15
	Mark the statement that is *too broad*	B	5
	Mark the statement that is *too narrow*	N	5

a. Antibiotics work by killing harmful bacteria that cause infectious diseases. ☐ _____

b. Penicillin affects reproducing bacteria. ☐ _____

c. Antibiotics include penicillin, ampicillin, and streptomycin. ☐ _____

Score 15 points for each correct answer.   **Score**

Subject Matter   2   The purpose of this passage is to
☐ a. introduce Alexander Fleming.
☐ b. explain the use of antibiotics in World War II.
☐ c. discuss antibiotics and the way they work.
☐ d. describe ampicillin and streptomycin.   _____

Supporting   3   Penicillin acts on bacteria by weakening
Details
☐ a. cell reproduction.
☐ b. the cell walls.
☐ c. their immune systems.
☐ d. protein development.   _____

Conclusion   4   From the last paragraph, we can conclude that
overprescription of antibiotics makes
☐ a. harmful bacteria resistant to the drugs.
☐ b. the drugs more effective.
☐ c. mutant bacteria weaker.
☐ d. new sources of antibiotics.   _____

Clarifying   5   The author begins this passage by
Devices
☐ a. defining penicillin.
☐ b. explaining cell division.
☐ c. contrasting the uses of antibiotics.
☐ d. describing the development of penicillin.   _____

Vocabulary   6   In this passage, <u>resistance</u> means
in Context
☐ a. the opposing troops during World War II.
☐ b. weakness.
☐ c. the ability not to be affected by.
☐ d. assist.   _____

Add your scores for questions 1–6. Enter the total here   **Total**
and on the graph on page 160.   **Score**   _____

66 A Multiuse Substance

Think of all the things around you that are made of glass; windows, containers, cookware, lightbulbs, eyeglasses, and decorative pieces are just a few possibilities. Glass is a hard, transparent material with a lustrous appearance and great durability. Such physical properties make glass very popular, but the chemical properties of glass are what allow us to fashion the various sizes, shapes, thicknesses, and colors needed to produce such a wide range of commonplace glass commodities.

Glass is made by heating a mixture of solid materials, such as sodium carbonate, limestone, and sand (silicon dioxide) until the atoms of the raw materials react. Some of the sand reacts with the limestone to form calcium silicate and carbon dioxide; the rest of the sand reacts with the sodium carbonate. The result is a three-dimensional network of silicon-oxygen bonds that in the short range of a few atomic distances are arranged regularly but in the long range have no regular pattern. This atomic structure makes the substance soft and <u>pliable</u> as it gradually passes into the liquid state, at which point it can be blown, rolled, or pressed into just about any shape. As the liquid cools, it thickens until it forms a shiny, hard, and very brittle solid.

Commercial glasses are usually silicates of sodium and calcium, but other elements and compounds may be substituted to produce different kinds of glass. Optical glass and cut-glass tableware, for example, are composed of sand, potassium carbonate, and lead oxide. Colored glasses are produced with the addition of various metals: manganese for purple, chromium for green, cobalt and copper for blue, silver for yellow, selenium for red, and calcium fluoride for white. The pale-green color common to glass bottles comes from iron compounds in the sand.

Main Idea 1	Answer	Score
Mark the *main idea*	M	15
Mark the statement that is *too broad*	B	5
Mark the statement that is *too narrow*	N	5
a. Many items in our everyday world are made of glass.	☐	____
b. The atomic structure of glass makes it soft and pliable.	☐	____
c. Glass is a shiny, hard material that can be molded into various sizes and shapes.	☐	____

Subject Matter   **2**   This passage is mostly concerned with the
- ☐ a. commodities around us.
- ☐ b. chemical properties of glass.
- ☐ c. physical appearance of glass.
- ☐ d. chemical name for sand.   _____

Supporting Details   **3**   Glass is soft and pliable as a liquid but hard and brittle as a solid because
- ☐ a. glass is heated until it becomes a liquid.
- ☐ b. it breaks easily when dropped.
- ☐ c. its atoms do not have a regular pattern.
- ☐ d. glass can be molded into just about any shape.   _____

Conclusion   **4**   A piece of green cut glass probably would *not* contain
- ☐ a. calcium.
- ☐ b. chromium.
- ☐ c. potassium carbonate.
- ☐ d. lead oxide.   _____

Clarifying Devices   **5**   The progression in this passage is
- ☐ a. in chronological order.
- ☐ b. in spatial order.
- ☐ c. from the less familiar to the more familiar.
- ☐ d. from the more familiar to the less familiar.   _____

Vocabulary in Context   **6**   The word <u>pliable</u> means
- ☐ a. rigid.
- ☐ b. fixed.
- ☐ c. flexible.
- ☐ d. immovable.   _____

Add your scores for questions 1–6. Enter the total here and on the graph on page 160.   **Total Score**   _____

67 Infection Makers

Contraction of a viral disease such as a common cold, the flu, chicken pox, mumps, measles, mononucleosis, polio, or hepatitis is an inescapable part of life. In fact, every living thing—whether it's a plant, fungi, algae, protozoa, animal, or bacteria— can be infected by a type of virus specific to that organism. A virus is an infectious noncellular structure of genetic material, either DNA (deoxyribonucleic acid) or RNA (ribonucleic acid), that is usually surrounded by a protein coat. The sole purpose of a virus is to produce more viruses. A virus cannot, however, <u>multiply</u> or grow independently because a virus is not a cell. A virus must infect, or enter, a living cell (called a host) and use the host's cell structures to reproduce more viruses. Eventually the infected host cell releases the new viruses, and then the host cell usually dies. The released viruses go on to infect other cells.

When a virus infects one or more cells of a body tissue, the infection causes the synthesis and secretion of proteins called interferons. These proteins strengthen the cell membrane of adjacent healthy cells so the virus cannot penetrate those cells. Sometimes, however, the virus succeeds in spreading to "other" cells. Then the human immune system activates and starts killing the viruses outside the cells as well as any infected cells themselves. Eventually the virus is eliminated, and the organism returns to good health.

Vaccination is often the best protection against viral disease. A vaccine contains weakened or dead viruses that no longer cause the disease. Upon entering the body, a vaccine triggers the immune system to produce antibodies that kill the weakened viruses. Vaccination often results in a lifelong immunity against further infection.

Main Idea 1 ————————————————————————

	Answer	Score
Mark the *main idea*	M	15
Mark the statement that is *too broad*	B	5
Mark the statement that is *too narrow*	N	5

a. A viral infection causes the secretion of proteins called interferons. ☐ _____

b. Viruses infect people by invading a host cell and reproducing, but then the body's immune system fights back ☐ _____

c. Viruses are structures that attack cells. ☐ _____

Subject Matter   **2**   The purpose of this passage is to
- ☐ a. define the role of interferons.
- ☐ b. explain the penetration of a host cell.
- ☐ c. describe the impact of a virus on a healthy organism.
- ☐ d. identify types of viral disease.

                                                           _____

Supporting Details   **3**   A virus cannot function independently because it
- ☐ a. has too much genetic material.
- ☐ b. is too small.
- ☐ c. usually kills the host cell.
- ☐ d. is not a cell with the structures necessary for growth and reproduction.

                                                             _____

Conclusion   **4**   We can conclude from the second paragraph that the "other" cells infected by the virus were
- ☐ a. not adjacent to the infected tissue.
- ☐ b. surrounded by a protein coat.
- ☐ c. synthesized and secreted proteins.
- ☐ d. killing the viruses outside the cells.

                                                             _____

Clarifying Devices   **5**   A device the author uses to help the reader understand the type of genetic material in a virus is
- ☐ a. quotation marks.
- ☐ b. parenthetical notes.
- ☐ c. a definition.
- ☐ d. an example.

                                                             _____

Vocabulary in Context   **6**   In this passage, the word <u>multiply</u> means
- ☐ a. live.
- ☐ b. reproduce.
- ☐ c. calculate.
- ☐ d. magnify.

                                                             _____

Add your scores for questions 1–6. Enter the total here and on the graph on page 160.   **Total Score**   _____

68 Seeing Double

Twinning, the process that leads to a multiple birth, takes place in the early stages of the reproductive process. The egg cell from the female and the sperm cell from the male are specialized cells called gametes, each of which contains one half of the genetic information needed to form a complete fetus. During fertilization, the female gamete and the male gamete unite to form a zygote, or a fertilized egg, that contains the combined genetic information from both parent cells.

When a zygote undergoes mitosis, or cell division, it splits into two (or more) parts that contain the exact genetic information. Each part develops into an embryo that is genetically identical to the other; the embryos are of the same sex. Since the separate embryos are formed from a single zygote, the identical twins are called monozygotic (MZ) twins. Usually MZ twins share a common placenta and amniotic sac.

When two separate zygotes are present to form two unique embryos, dizygotic (DZ) twins, or fraternal twins, form. The presence of two zygotes is a result of multiple ovulations within a single menstrual cycle. As part of the continued birth process, a placenta is formed for each zygote. Since DZ twins come from two separate zygotes, they are no more genetically similar than are other <u>siblings</u>. DZ twins do not have to be of the same sex.

Multiple births have increased since fertility drugs were introduced in the 1960s to help couples who have difficulty conceiving. Fertility drugs often cause the release of more than one egg from the ovary, thus increasing the chance of multiple births of DZ twins.

Main Idea 1 ——————————————————————————

	Answer	Score
Mark the *main idea*	M	15
Mark the statement that is *too broad*	B	5
Mark the statement that is *too narrow*	N	5

a. Whether twins are identical or fraternal depends on how many zygotes are present. ☐ _____

b. Monozygotic twins are genetically identical. ☐ _____

c. Twin births are fairly common occurrences. ☐ _____

Subject Matter   2   The purpose of this passage is to
- ☐ a. define *monozygotic* and *dizygotic*.
- ☐ b. explain the process of twinning.
- ☐ c. describe fertilization.
- ☐ d. discuss mitosis.

_____

Supporting Details   3   During twinning, the specific process that results in the formation of monozygotic twins is
- ☐ a. ovulation.
- ☐ b. mitosis.
- ☐ c. reproduction.
- ☐ d. fertilization.

_____

Conclusion   4   If the prefix *mono* in *monozygotic* means "one," then the prefix *di* in *dizygotic* must mean
- ☐ a. multiple.
- ☐ b. two.
- ☐ c. split in half.
- ☐ d. a choice.

_____

Clarifying Devices   5   To help the reader understand why identical and fraternal twins are different, the writer
- ☐ a. describes the union of the two gametes.
- ☐ b. explains monozygotic twinning and then dizygotic twinning.
- ☐ c. contrasts fertilization and mitosis.
- ☐ d. discusses the effects of fertility drugs.

_____

Vocabulary in Context   6   The word <u>siblings</u> means
- ☐ a. split personalities.
- ☐ b. female and male gametes.
- ☐ c. the genetic relationship between twins.
- ☐ d. brothers and sisters.

_____

Add your scores for questions 1–6. Enter the total here and on the graph on page 160.   **Total Score**   _____

69 A Chain of Life

The organisms in a community have a common link in that each organism is food for the next. A food chain shows the transfer of energy from one organism to another in a community. The chain begins with producers that make their own food. Green plants, for example, are producers that obtain chemical energy through photosynthesis. During photosynthesis green plants transform the sun's radiant energy into the chemical energy that plants use for life. The energy in the green plants is transferred to other organisms in the community when consumers, or organisms that cannot produce their own food, feed on the plants and obtain the energy and nutrients stored in them. All animals are consumers, because they must eat green plants or other animals to obtain energy. When a producer or a consumer dies, its body <u>decomposes</u> into minerals and gases that are then used by plants when they convert the sun's radiant energy into chemical energy. Thus another food chain begins in the community.

Scientists, after closely examining food chains, have found that toxic chemicals, such as some pesticides and herbicides that are sprayed in an environment, can be passed through a food chain. The toxins build up in a consumer's body as the consumer eats more contaminated food, which may be producers, consumers, or both. Eventually in a process called biological magnification, high concentrations of poison accumulate in the bodies of consumers and kill them. Since humans have a very long life span of eating plants and animals from food chains, there is serious concern that we are likely to experience biological magnification. Some doctors who have seen an increase in the types and numbers of cancers striking children and young adults believe that humans already are being affected by toxic chemicals in food chains.

Main Idea 1	Answer	Score
Mark the _main idea_	M	15
Mark the statement that is _too broad_	B	5
Mark the statement that is _too narrow_	N	5

a. Organisms in a community transfer energy by feeding off one another, but they may also pass contaminants. ☐ _____

b. Consumers eat producers or other consumers. ☐ _____

c. Food chains are of interest to scientists. ☐ _____

Score 15 points for each correct answer.   **Score**

Subject Matter   2   The primary purpose of this passage is to
- [ ] a. define photosynthesis.
- [ ] b. explain biological magnification.
- [ ] c. describe the workings of a food chain.
- [ ] d. tell about man-made influences that can be transferred through a food chain.

_____

Supporting Details   3   Consumers in a food chain
- [ ] a. cannot produce their own food.
- [ ] b. obtain chemical energy through photosynthesis.
- [ ] c. do not experience biological magnification.
- [ ] d. are mostly pesticides.

_____

Conclusion   4   The author's tone at the end of this article shows
- [ ] a. no feelings.
- [ ] b. amusement.
- [ ] c. anger.
- [ ] d. concern.

_____

Clarifying Devices   5   The first paragraph of this selection
- [ ] a. compares and contrasts.
- [ ] b. explains a process.
- [ ] c. narrates an episode.
- [ ] d. persuades through facts and details.

_____

Vocabulary in Context   6   Another word for <u>decomposes</u> is
- [ ] a. decays.
- [ ] b. reproduces.
- [ ] c. doubles.
- [ ] d. generates.

_____

Add your scores for questions 1–6. Enter the total here and on the graph on page 160.   **Total Score**

_____

70 Real-World Robots

When you think of a robot, do you envision a shiny metallic device having the same general shape as a human being, performing humanlike functions, and responding to your questions in a monotone voice accentuated by high-pitched tones and beeps? This is the way many of us imagine a robot, but in the real world a robot is not <u>humanoid</u> at all. Instead a robot often is a voiceless box-shaped machine that efficiently carries out repetitive or dangerous functions usually performed by humans. Today's robot is more than an automatic machine that performs one task again and again. A modern robot is programmed with varying degrees of artificial intelligence—that is, a robot contains a computer program that tells it how to perform tasks associated with human intelligence, such as reasoning, drawing conclusions, and learning from past experience.

A robot does not possess a human shape for the simple reason that a two-legged robot has great difficulty remaining balanced. A robot does, however, move from place to place on wheels and axles that roll and rotate. A robot even has limbs that swivel and move in combination with joints and motors. To find its way in its surroundings, a robot utilizes various built-in sensors. Antennae attached to the robot's base detect anything they bump into. If the robot starts to teeter as it moves on an incline, a gyroscope or a pendulum inside it senses the vertical differential. To determine its distance from an object and how quickly it will reach the object, the robot bounces laser beams and ultrasonic sound waves off obstructions in its path. These and other sensors constantly feed information to the computer, which then analyzes the information and corrects or adjusts the robot's actions. As science and technology advance, the robot too will advance in its ability to use artificial-intelligence programs.

Main Idea	1		
		Answer	**Score**
Mark the *main idea*		M	15
Mark the statement that is *too broad*		B	5
Mark the statement that is *too narrow*		N	5

a. A robot, aided by artificial intelligence, can perform certain human functions. ☐ _____

b. Today's robots move on wheels and axles. ☐ _____

c. Robots can be useful to people. ☐ _____

Score 15 points for each correct answer. Score

Subject Matter 2 Another good title for this passage would be
☐ a. Robots: Taking the Place of Humans.
☐ b. Artificial Intelligence Programs.
☐ c. Today's Robots and How They Function.
☐ d. Modern-Day Sensors. _____

Supporting 3 Artificial intelligence is
Details
☐ a. the unnatural way in which robots move.
☐ b. a voiceless box-shaped machine that performs repetitive tasks.
☐ c. sensors such as antennae and a gyroscope.
☐ d. a computer program that imitates human intellectual processes. _____

Conclusion 4 The last paragraph suggests that future robots will be
☐ a. more humanlike in behavior and actions.
☐ b. more like automatic machines.
☐ c. better able to move on inclines.
☐ d. better equipped with laser light sensors. _____

Clarifying 5 The writer begins the passage by comparing
Devices
☐ a. the shape of a human being with a box.
☐ b. a modern robot with a fictional robot.
☐ c. an imaginary machine with a human.
☐ d. a computer program with artificial intelligence. _____

Vocabulary 6 The word <u>humanoid</u> means
in Context
☐ a. lacking human characteristics.
☐ b. anything having the appearance of a humanoid.
☐ c. being void or vacant.
☐ d. having a human form or characteristics. _____

Add your scores for questions 1–6. Enter the total here Total
and on the graph on page 160. Score _____

71 Water to Drink

We need water for drinking, bathing, cleaning, and numerous other purposes. But how can we be certain that the water we drink and use is safe? Communities operate water-treatment plants to remove contaminants, harmful microorganisms, and chemicals and to render the water crystal clear, with almost no color, odor, or taste.

Any number of physical and chemical processes can be used to treat water for domestic use. Water entering a water-treatment plant passes through *screening* to remove fish, dead leaves, and other large objects. Then the water undergoes various processes to eliminate impurities that are suspended, or mixed but not dissolved, in the water and to improve its clarity. During *coagulation* and *flocculation,* a chemical coagulant such as aluminum sulfate, ferric sulfate, or sodium aluminate is added to the water to bring small suspended particles together into larger, heavier masses called floc. Next, the water goes through the processes of *clarification* and *sedimentation.* The water, filled with floc and other particles, flows into sedimentation tanks. As the water stands immobile in the tanks, the floc and other dense particles settle to the bottom. The clarified water at the top is then skimmed off, but this water still contains impurities. These are removed through *filtration.* In this step, water trickles downward through layers of a filter. Layers made up of anthracite coal, sand, and gravel trap most of the remaining suspended particles. A final process involves *disinfection,* which destroys any disease-carrying microbes in the water. This step is accomplished either by applying chlorine or ozone to the water or by exposing the water to ultraviolet radiation. At this point, other processes such as softening, aeration, and fluoridation may be performed to meet a community's drinking water standards.

Main Idea	1	Answer	Score
	Mark the *main idea*	M	15
	Mark the statement that is *too broad*	B	5
	Mark the statement that is *too narrow*	N	5

a. Water treatment involves processes that make water suitable for drinking. ☐ _____

b. During filtration, water trickles downward through layers of a filter. ☐ _____

c. We need water for many purposes in our lives. ☐ _____

Score 15 points for each correct answer. **Score**

Subject Matter   **2**   Another good title for this passage would be
☐ a. Harmful Microorganisms in Our Water.
☐ b. Getting the Lumps Out of Water.
☐ c. What Happens at Water Treatment Plants.
☐ d. Microbes Are Trickling from Your Faucet.   _____

Supporting   **3**   A chemical coagulant causes
Details
☐ a. large objects to become trapped.
☐ b. sediment to stand still in the tank.
☐ c. disease-carrying microbes to be destroyed.
☐ d. particles in the water to clump together.   _____

Conclusion   **4**   We can conclude that we should not
☐ a. drink tap water unless it has been processed
at a water treatment plant.
☐ b. care whether water has been processed at a
water treatment plant.
☐ c. apply ozone to our drinking water.
☐ d. use physical and chemical processes to treat
our drinking water.   _____

Clarifying   **5**   To help the reader identify the processes that
Devices   purify our drinking water, the author
☐ a. defines each process.
☐ b. explains flocculation.
☐ c. italicizes the terms.
☐ d. describes filtration.   _____

Vocabulary   **6**   The word <u>clarity</u> means
in Context
☐ a. smell.
☐ b. clearness.
☐ c. taste.
☐ d. color.   _____

Add your scores for questions 1–6. Enter the total here   **Total**
and on the graph on page 160.   **Score**   _____

72 Polymers

We use polymers to make such goods as telephones, television screens, computers, fabrics, combs, baby bottles, carpets, CDs, automobile bumpers, asphalt roads, dishes, artificial body parts, insulation, and pesticides. Each of these products contains synthetic polymers; that is, each is made partly or entirely of substances such as plastic, nylon, acrylic, or silicone. Though some polymers—starch, cotton, rubber, leather, and DNA, for instance—exist naturally, a great many others are synthetic.

In scientific terms, polymers are large molecules made of smaller molecules <u>bonded</u> together. Polymers exist because of a remarkable element—carbon. Atoms of carbon form very strong three-dimensional bonds with other carbon atoms as well as with atoms of hydrogen, oxygen, nitrogen, sulfur, phosphorus, and many other elements. Carbon's unique bonding enables the atoms to combine in varied ways, literally forming millions of different carbon compounds. A polymer results when some of these smaller carbon compounds bond together in long chains, sometimes forming a polymer molecule of hundreds of atoms.

A polymer chemist is a scientist who studies carbon compounds and their properties. The chemist identifies the number and types of atoms in a compound and the pattern in which the atoms bond. Then he or she conducts experiments to observe the compound's reaction to heat and other substances. Through such studies, the chemist discovers how to synthesize molecules with specific desired properties. Chemists have used such procedures to synthesize polymers that vary in hardness, flexibility, softening temperature, and biodegradability. Due to the work of polymer chemists, we are able to use polymers to create numerous indispensable products.

Main Idea	1	Answer	Score
	Mark the *main idea*	M	15
	Mark the statement that is *too broad*	B	5
	Mark the statement that is *too narrow*	N	5

a. Carbon's bonding enables atoms to form millions of carbon compounds. ☐ _____

b. Polymers are used in many products. ☐ _____

c. Synthetic polymers can be created to fulfill specific needs. ☐ _____

Subject Matter   **2**   Another good title for this passage would be
- ☐ a. The Properties of Plastics.
- ☐ b. The Many Uses of Nylon.
- ☐ c. What Is Silicone?
- ☐ d. Creating Polymers.   _____

Supporting Details   **3**   A polymer molecule contains
- ☐ a. carbon compounds.
- ☐ b. never more than a few atoms.
- ☐ c. asphalt.
- ☐ d. a combination of natural and synthetic fibers.   _____

Conclusion   **4**   When polymer chemists first began their studies, they most likely experimented with
- ☐ a. nylon materials.
- ☐ b. pesticides.
- ☐ c. natural polymers.
- ☐ d. synthetic polymers.   _____

Clarifying Devices   **5**   The author introduces the topic by presenting
- ☐ a. detailed word pictures.
- ☐ b. scientific studies.
- ☐ c. several different facts.
- ☐ d. specific examples.   _____

Vocabulary in Context   **6**   In this passage, the word <u>bonded</u> means
- ☐ a. obligated.
- ☐ b. paroled.
- ☐ c. released.
- ☐ d. joined.   _____

Add your scores for questions 1–6. Enter the total here and on the graph on page 160.   **Total Score**   _____

73 Helpful or Harmful?

Radiation in one form or another is part of our everyday lives. Cosmic rays from outer space, radiation from the sun, radioactive elements in the earth's crust, and electromagnetic radiation from radio waves, television sets, and electricity are sources of "background radiation." The long-term effects of radiation exposure are not fully known. But a branch of science called radiation biology is focused on finding out.

Radiation biologists study the effects of radiation on living tissue. The need for such studies became clear after atomic bombs were dropped on Japan during World War II. The biological effects of exposure to such large amounts of radiation were <u>devastating</u> to thousands of war survivors. High doses of radiation disrupt the molecular structure of a body's tissues. These molecular changes trigger a chain of events that can produce gene damage and cell mutations. The results include birth defects, tumors, eye cataracts, brain convulsions, nausea, and other injuries.

Radiation biologists believe, however, that small amounts of radiation exposure are of greater benefit than harm. Medical science, for example, commonly uses small amounts of radiation to diagnose and treat disease. Radioactive iodine helps doctors to diagnose thyroid problems. Radioactive isotopes let doctors trace the path of food molecules through the digestive system. Radiology procedures assist doctors in detecting tumors, brain activity, weakened heart muscle, and other conditions. Such procedures include the use of x-rays, PET (positron emission tomography) scans, CAT (computerized axial tomography) scans, and MRI (magnetic resonance imaging). As long as exposure to radiation is carefully controlled, people's lives can be prolonged rather than destroyed.

Main Idea	1		Answer	Score
	Mark the *main idea*		M	15
	Mark the statement that is *too broad*		B	5
	Mark the statement that is *too narrow*		N	5
	a. Radiation is all around us.		☐	_____
	b. Radiation biologists have learned that radiation can be helpful as well as harmful.		☐	_____
	c. High doses of radiation disrupt the molecular structure of a body's tissues.		☐	_____

Score 15 points for each correct answer.   **Score**

Subject Matter   **2**   Another good title for this passage would be
☐ a. Radioactive Elements on Earth.
☐ b. Radiation Exposure During World War II.
☐ c. Types of Radiation.
☐ d. The Pros and Cons of Radiation.   _____

Supporting Details   **3**   Birth defects, tumors, eye cataracts, and other disorders are the result of
☐ a. exposure to background radiation.
☐ b. changes in the molecular structure of tissue.
☐ c. MRIs.
☐ d. radiology procedures such as x-rays, CAT scans, PET scans, and MRI.   _____

Conclusion   **4**   This passage suggests that radiation from the atomic bombs dropped in Japan
☐ a. had very little effect on people.
☐ b. was harmful only.
☐ c. was both helpful and harmful.
☐ d. was helpful only.   _____

Clarifying Devices   **5**   In the first paragraph, the term *background radiation* means
☐ a. the long-term effects of radiation.
☐ b. the effects of radiation on living tissue.
☐ c. a fairly steady radiation level in the environment.
☐ d. a molecular change from radiation exposure.   _____

Vocabulary in Context   **6**   Another word for <u>devastating</u> is
☐ a. ruinous.
☐ b. restorative.
☐ c. wholesome.
☐ d. beneficial.   _____

Add your scores for questions 1–6. Enter the total here   **Total**
and on the graph on page 160.   **Score**   _____

74 Forever Warm

Environmental scientists continue to issue warnings about global warming, or the possible increase in average global atmospheric temperatures. Is there any legitimate concern about the earth's temperature rising a few degrees? In fact, a surface temperature increase of just a few degrees could lead to a partial melting of the polar icecaps, resulting in a major rise in sea levels. Some scientists predict that by the middle of the 21st century sea levels could rise by three or more feet. If sea levels rise as expected, coastal areas or tidal cities, such as New York and London, as well as of the best low-lying agricultural areas would experience regular flooding. In Bangladesh, where the Ganges River reaches the sea, such flooding could <u>displace</u> 15 million people. Scientists also believe that global warming may cause more frequent extreme weather patterns. Stronger winds, more destructive hurricanes, and particularly devastating droughts would become normal events. The major climatic zones may also shift, thus affecting some of the most fertile and productive agricultural areas on earth.

Global warming is caused when heat radiated by the earth's surface becomes trapped in the lower atmosphere by gases, such as water vapor (H_2O), carbon dioxide (CO_2), and methane (CH_4), and is reradiated back to the earth's surface, thereby warming it. Although some of this "greenhouse effect" occurs naturally in the atmosphere, the effect intensifies as atmospheric greenhouse gases increase. Human actions, such as the burning of fossil fuels and the destruction of tropical rain forests, add to the greenhouse gases, particularly carbon dioxide, in the atmosphere and thus increase the warming of the earth's surface. If global warming occurs as many scientists predict, the repercussions will be severe for ecosystems and human populations on earth.

Main Idea	1		Answer	Score
	Mark the *main idea*		M	15
	Mark the statement that is *too broad*		B	5
	Mark the statement that is *too narrow*		N	5
	a. Global warming may very well happen.	☐		____
	b. Global warming may have severe repercussions for the entire earth.	☐		____
	c. Sea levels could rise by three or more feet by the middle of the 21st century.	☐		____

Subject Matter   **2**   This passage is concerned with the
- ☐ a. scientists who study earth's environment.
- ☐ b. polar icecaps and why they melt.
- ☐ c. regular flooding of coastal areas.
- ☐ d. consequences of the increase in average atmospheric temperatures around the earth.   _____

Supporting Details   **3**   Some scientists predict that in 50 years,
- ☐ a. there will be no winter weather on earth.
- ☐ b. the earth will be uninhabitable.
- ☐ c. seas could rise three or more feet.
- ☐ d. New York City and London will disappear.   _____

Conclusion   **4**   The effects of global warming as described in this passage
- ☐ a. seem likely to happen.
- ☐ b. are certain to happen.
- ☐ c. are based on faulty ideas.
- ☐ d. cannot be prevented at this late date.   _____

Clarifying Devices   **5**   The writer presents "greenhouse effect" by
- ☐ a. explaining the chemical names of the gases.
- ☐ b. giving an explanation of the process.
- ☐ c. listing the results of careful measurements.
- ☐ d. defining the major climatic zones.   _____

Vocabulary in Context   **6**   In this passage, the word <u>displace</u> means to
- ☐ a. incur the disapproval of.
- ☐ b. force to flee from home.
- ☐ c. put in a particular position.
- ☐ d. restore to a former position.   _____

Add your scores for questions 1–6. Enter the total here and on the graph on page 160.   **Total Score**   _____

75 Keep Those Teeth Clean!

You probably are aware of proper dental hygiene practices such as those taught to children: to brush the teeth at least twice daily, to floss every day, to eat nutritious foods, and to have teeth professionally cleaned twice a year. Proper oral hygiene is important for preventing periodontal disease, or gum disease, caused by different types of bacteria that reside in the mouth. When bacteria are allowed to develop and strengthen, high levels of toxins are produced, and infection and <u>inflammation</u> of the gums follow. This inflammation of the gums, marked by redness and bleeding, is called gingivitis. It is the first stage of periodontal disease. If not properly treated, gingivitis can progress to a more advanced gum disease known as periodontitis, or pyorrhea, in which the gum tissues and bone that support the teeth dissolve, eventually leading to tooth loss.

Proper brushing and flossing remove some bacteria from the mouth and ensure that the remaining bacteria cannot progress to dangerous levels. When brushing and flossing are absent from daily dental care, plaque—a sticky yellow-white film consisting of bacteria, small particles, proteins, and mucus—accumulates on the gums and teeth. Over time, plaque mineralizes and calcifies, or hardens, into tartar, and then it cannot be removed by brushing or flossing.

Prevention of and treatments for periodontal disease range from simple cleaning and scaling to painful and expensive surgical procedures that may involve cutting the gums away from the teeth to remove deeply imbedded bacteria, replacing lost bone tissue, performing gum grafts, and bonding the teeth together for increased stability. So which situation is more sensible—prevention now or treatment later?

Main Idea 1

	Answer	Score
Mark the *main idea*	M	15
Mark the statement that is *too broad*	B	5
Mark the statement that is *too narrow*	N	5

a. Proper oral hygiene includes brushing, flossing, and professional teeth cleaning. ☐ _____

b. Periodontal disease is often a serious problem. ☐ _____

c. Periodontal disease occurs in different stages and has varying treatments. ☐ _____

Subject Matter   **2**   The purpose of this passage is to
- □ a. describe types of bacteria in the mouth.
- □ b. discuss the causes and treatment of periodontal disease.
- □ c. explain plaque and tartar.
- □ d. compare gingivitis with periodontitis.   _____

Supporting Details   **3**   The early stage of periodontal disease is called
- □ a. gingivitis.
- □ b. plaque.
- □ c. periodontitis.
- □ d. tartar.   _____

Conclusion   **4**   In the last sentence of the passage, the author suggests that if you suffer from periodontal disease,
- □ a. the cost and pain involved will be great.
- □ b. you have no one to blame but yourself.
- □ c. the gums will become inflamed and reddened.
- □ d. your teeth will loosen due to bone loss.   _____

Clarifying Devices   **5**   The first two paragraphs are developed primarily through
- □ a. defining terms in order of importance.
- □ b. using various persuasive techniques.
- □ c. describing the stages in a process.
- □ d. presenting questions and answers.   _____

Vocabulary in Context   **6**   In this passage, <u>inflammation</u> means
- □ a. a reddened, diseased condition.
- □ b. the state of bursting into flames.
- □ c. a lessening of infection.
- □ d. a treatment for disease.   _____

Add your scores for questions 1–6. Enter the total here and on the graph on page 160.   **Total Score**   _____

Answer Key: Passages 1–25

Passage 1:	1a. **M**	1b. **B**	1c. **N**	2. **a**	3. **d**	4. **c**	5. **d**	6. **a**
Passage 2:	1a. **B**	1b. **M**	1c. **N**	2. **d**	3. **b**	4. **c**	5. **a**	6. **a**
Passage 3:	1a. **N**	1b. **M**	1c. **B**	2. **c**	3. **b**	4. **a**	5. **c**	6. **b**
Passage 4:	1a. **N**	1b. **B**	1c. **M**	2. **c**	3. **a**	4. **b**	5. **d**	6. **d**
Passage 5:	1a. **M**	1b. **N**	1c. **B**	2. **d**	3. **c**	4. **a**	5. **b**	6. **a**
Passage 6:	1a. **M**	1b. **B**	1c. **N**	2. **c**	3. **d**	4. **b**	5. **a**	6. **d**
Passage 7:	1a. **N**	1b. **B**	1c. **M**	2. **c**	3. **b**	4. **d**	5. **b**	6. **c**
Passage 8:	1a. **N**	1b. **M**	1c. **B**	2. **d**	3. **c**	4. **a**	5. **b**	6. **c**
Passage 9:	1a. **B**	1b. **N**	1c. **M**	2. **d**	3. **a**	4. **a**	5. **c**	6. **b**
Passage 10:	1a. **B**	1b. **N**	1c. **M**	2. **b**	3. **a**	4. **d**	5. **c**	6. **b**
Passage 11:	1a. **M**	1b. **B**	1c. **N**	2. **a**	3. **c**	4. **d**	5. **c**	6. **b**
Passage 12:	1a. **N**	1b. **B**	1c. **M**	2. **a**	3. **c**	4. **d**	5. **c**	6. **b**
Passage 13:	1a. **N**	1b. **B**	1c. **M**	2. **a**	3. **d**	4. **b**	5. **b**	6. **a**
Passage 14:	1a. **M**	1b. **B**	1c. **N**	2. **d**	3. **a**	4. **b**	5. **c**	6. **a**
Passage 15:	1a. **N**	1b. **B**	1c. **M**	2. **b**	3. **d**	4. **a**	5. **c**	6. **b**
Passage 16:	1a. **M**	1b. **N**	1c. **B**	2. **c**	3. **b**	4. **c**	5. **a**	6. **a**
Passage 17:	1a. **B**	1b. **N**	1c. **M**	2. **b**	3. **a**	4. **c**	5. **d**	6. **d**
Passage 18:	1a. **B**	1b. **M**	1c. **N**	2. **a**	3. **c**	4. **d**	5. **b**	6. **b**
Passage 19:	1a. **B**	1b. **N**	1c. **M**	2. **c**	3. **a**	4. **b**	5. **d**	6. **a**
Passage 20:	1a. **B**	1b. **N**	1c. **M**	2. **c**	3. **b**	4. **d**	5. **b**	6. **b**
Passage 21:	1a. **N**	1b. **B**	1c. **M**	2. **c**	3. **d**	4. **a**	5. **c**	6. **a**
Passage 22:	1a. **B**	1b. **N**	1c. **M**	2. **b**	3. **a**	4. **d**	5. **a**	6. **c**
Passage 23:	1a. **M**	1b. **N**	1c. **B**	2. **d**	3. **d**	4. **b**	5. **a**	6. **d**
Passage 24:	1a. **B**	1b. **N**	1c. **M**	2. **c**	3. **a**	4. **c**	5. **a**	6. **b**
Passage 25:	1a. **B**	1b. **M**	1c. **N**	2. **a**	3. **a**	4. **b**	5. **b**	6. **d**

Answer Key: Passages 26–50

Passage 26:	1a. **B**	1b. **N**	1c. **M**	2. **b**	3. **b**	4. **a**	5. **a**	6. **c**
Passage 27:	1a. **M**	1b. **N**	1c. **B**	2. **a**	3. **d**	4. **a**	5. **d**	6. **c**
Passage 28:	1a. **N**	1b. **B**	1c. **M**	2. **c**	3. **d**	4. **a**	5. **a**	6. **b**
Passage 29:	1a. **B**	1b. **M**	1c. **N**	2. **b**	3. **b**	4. **b**	5. **a**	6. **d**
Passage 30:	1a. **N**	1b. **M**	1c. **B**	2. **b**	3. **d**	4. **a**	5. **b**	6. **c**
Passage 31:	1a. **B**	1b. **M**	1c. **N**	2. **a**	3. **a**	4. **d**	5. **c**	6. **c**
Passage 32:	1a. **N**	1b. **M**	1c. **B**	2. **c**	3. **c**	4. **b**	5. **c**	6. **a**
Passage 33:	1a. **B**	1b. **N**	1c. **M**	2. **c**	3. **a**	4. **c**	5. **a**	6. **d**
Passage 34:	1a. **B**	1b. **N**	1c. **M**	2. **a**	3. **a**	4. **c**	5. **b**	6. **a**
Passage 35:	1a. **B**	1b. **N**	1c. **M**	2. **a**	3. **b**	4. **b**	5. **c**	6. **b**
Passage 36:	1a. **N**	1b. **B**	1c. **M**	2. **d**	3. **c**	4. **c**	5. **b**	6. **a**
Passage 37:	1a. **N**	1b. **M**	1c. **B**	2. **a**	3. **c**	4. **b**	5. **a**	6. **d**
Passage 38:	1a. **N**	1b. **M**	1c. **B**	2. **c**	3. **b**	4. **c**	5. **a**	6. **c**
Passage 39:	1a. **M**	1b. **N**	1c. **B**	2. **d**	3. **c**	4. **a**	5. **b**	6. **c**
Passage 40:	1a. **B**	1b. **M**	1c. **N**	2. **a**	3. **c**	4. **b**	5. **a**	6. **a**
Passage 41:	1a. **M**	1b. **B**	1c. **N**	2. **b**	3. **a**	4. **d**	5. **b**	6. **a**
Passage 42:	1a. **N**	1b. **B**	1c. **M**	2. **a**	3. **b**	4. **b**	5. **a**	6. **c**
Passage 43:	1a. **B**	1b. **M**	1c. **N**	2. **d**	3. **c**	4. **a**	5. **b**	6. **d**
Passage 44:	1a. **B**	1b. **N**	1c. **M**	2. **a**	3. **b**	4. **c**	5. **d**	6. **c**
Passage 45:	1a. **M**	1b. **B**	1c. **N**	2. **d**	3. **c**	4. **b**	5. **c**	6. **a**
Passage 46:	1a. **B**	1b. **M**	1c. **N**	2. **c**	3. **a**	4. **c**	5. **a**	6. **d**
Passage 47:	1a. **N**	1b. **B**	1c. **M**	2. **d**	3. **c**	4. **a**	5. **c**	6. **c**
Passage 48:	1a. **B**	1b. **N**	1c. **M**	2. **c**	3. **d**	4. **a**	5. **a**	6. **b**
Passage 49:	1a. **B**	1b. **M**	1c. **N**	2. **d**	3. **a**	4. **a**	5. **c**	6. **c**
Passage 50:	1a. **M**	1b. **B**	1c. **N**	2. **b**	3. **b**	4. **a**	5. **c**	6. **d**

Answer Key: Passages 51–75

Passage 51:   1a. **M**   1b. **B**   1c. **N**   2. **c**   3. **d**   4. **b**   5. **a**   6. **b**

Passage 52:   1a. **B**   1b. **M**   1c. **N**   2. **b**   3. **d**   4. **a**   5. **b**   6. **d**

Passage 53:   1a. **M**   1b. **B**   1c. **N**   2. **d**   3. **a**   4. **c**   5. **a**   6. **b**

Passage 54:   1a. **N**   1b. **B**   1c. **M**   2. **d**   3. **c**   4. **b**   5. **a**   6. **d**

Passage 55:   1a. **B**   1b. **N**   1c. **M**   2. **b**   3. **d**   4. **a**   5. **c**   6. **a**

Passage 56:   1a. **N**   1b. **B**   1c. **M**   2. **a**   3. **c**   4. **a**   5. **b**   6. **b**

Passage 57:   1a. **M**   1b. **B**   1c. **N**   2. **b**   3. **a**   4. **a**   5. **c**   6. **a**

Passage 58:   1a. **N**   1b. **B**   1c. **M**   2. **a**   3. **c**   4. **b**   5. **a**   6. **c**

Passage 59:   1a. **M**   1b. **N**   1c. **B**   2. **b**   3. **d**   4. **d**   5. **a**   6. **d**

Passage 60:   1a. **B**   1b. **M**   1c. **N**   2. **d**   3. **a**   4. **b**   5. **d**   6. **c**

Passage 61:   1a. **N**   1b. **M**   1c. **B**   2. **d**   3. **a**   4. **b**   5. **a**   6. **b**

Passage 62:   1a. **B**   1b. **N**   1c. **M**   2. **c**   3. **b**   4. **d**   5. **a**   6. **b**

Passage 63:   1a. **M**   1b. **B**   1c. **N**   2. **c**   3. **d**   4. **a**   5. **d**   6. **b**

Passage 64:   1a. **B**   1b. **N**   1c. **M**   2. **b**   3. **b**   4. **a**   5. **a**   6. **a**

Passage 65:   1a. **M**   1b. **N**   1c. **B**   2. **c**   3. **b**   4. **a**   5. **d**   6. **c**

Passage 66:   1a. **B**   1b. **N**   1c. **M**   2. **b**   3. **c**   4. **a**   5. **d**   6. **c**

Passage 67:   1a. **N**   1b. **M**   1c. **B**   2. **c**   3. **d**   4. **a**   5. **b**   6. **b**

Passage 68:   1a. **M**   1b. **N**   1c. **B**   2. **b**   3. **b**   4. **b**   5. **b**   6. **d**

Passage 69:   1a. **M**   1b. **N**   1c. **B**   2. **c**   3. **a**   4. **d**   5. **b**   6. **a**

Passage 70:   1a. **M**   1b. **N**   1c. **B**   2. **c**   3. **d**   4. **a**   5. **b**   6. **d**

Passage 71:   1a. **M**   1b. **N**   1c. **B**   2. **c**   3. **d**   4. **a**   5. **c**   6. **b**

Passage 72:   1a. **N**   1b. **B**   1c. **M**   2. **d**   3. **a**   4. **c**   5. **d**   6. **d**

Passage 73:   1a. **B**   1b. **M**   1c. **N**   2. **d**   3. **b**   4. **b**   5. **c**   6. **a**

Passage 74:   1a. **B**   1b. **M**   1c. **N**   2. **d**   3. **c**   4. **a**   5. **b**   6. **b**

Passage 75:   1a. **N**   1b. **B**   1c. **M**   2. **b**   3. **a**   4. **b**   5. **c**   6. **a**

Diagnostic Chart: Passages 1–25

Directions: For each passage, write your answers to the left of the dotted line in the blocks for each skill category. Then correct your answers using the Answer Key on page 152. If your answer is correct, do not make any more marks in the block. If your answer is incorrect, write the letter of the correct answer to the right of the dotted line.

	Categories of Comprehension Skills								
	1 Main Idea			2	3	4	5	6	
	Statement a	Statement b	Statement c	Subject Matter	Supporting Details	Conclusion	Clarifying Devices	Vocabulary in Context	
Passage 1									
Passage 2									
Passage 3									
Passage 4									
Passage 5									
Passage 6									
Passage 7									
Passage 8									
Passage 9									
Passage 10									
Passage 11									
Passage 12									
Passage 13									
Passage 14									
Passage 15									
Passage 16									
Passage 17									
Passage 18									
Passage 19									
Passage 20									
Passage 21									
Passage 22									
Passage 23									
Passage 24									
Passage 25									

Diagnostic Chart: Passages 26–50

Directions: For each passage, write your answers to the left of the dotted line in the blocks for each skill category. Then correct your answers using the Answer Key on page 153. If your answer is correct, do not make any more marks in the block. If your answer is incorrect, write the letter of the correct answer to the right of the dotted line.

	Categories of Comprehension Skills								
	1 Main Idea			2	3	4	5	6	
	Statement a	Statement b	Statement c	Subject Matter	Supporting Details	Conclusion	Clarifying Devices	Vocabulary in Context	
Passage 26									
Passage 27									
Passage 28									
Passage 29									
Passage 30									
Passage 31									
Passage 32									
Passage 33									
Passage 34									
Passage 35									
Passage 36									
Passage 37									
Passage 38									
Passage 39									
Passage 40									
Passage 41									
Passage 42									
Passage 43									
Passage 44									
Passage 45									
Passage 46									
Passage 47									
Passage 48									
Passage 49									
Passage 50									

Diagnostic Chart: Passages 51–75

Directions: For each passage, write your answers to the left of the dotted line in the blocks for each skill category. Then correct your answers using the Answer Key on page 154. If your answer is correct, do not make any more marks in the block. If your answer is incorrect, write the letter of the correct answer to the right of the dotted line.

	Categories of Comprehension Skills								
	1 Main Idea			**2**	**3**	**4**	**5**	**6**	
	Statement a	Statement b	Statement c	Subject Matter	Supporting Details	Conclusion	Clarifying Devices	Vocabulary in Context	
Passage 51									
Passage 52									
Passage 53									
Passage 54									
Passage 55									
Passage 56									
Passage 57									
Passage 58									
Passage 59									
Passage 60									
Passage 61									
Passage 62									
Passage 63									
Passage 64									
Passage 65									
Passage 66									
Passage 67									
Passage 68									
Passage 69									
Passage 70									
Passage 71									
Passage 72									
Passage 73									
Passage 74									
Passage 75									

Progress Graph: Passages 1–25

Directions: Write your Total Score for each passage in the comprehension score box under the number of the passage. Then plot your score on the graph itself by putting a small *x* on the line directly above the number of the passage, across from the score you got for that passage. As you mark your score for each passage, graph your progress by drawing a line to connect the *x*'s.

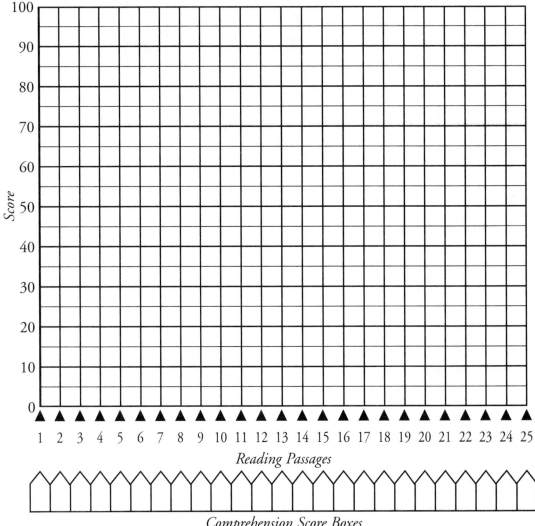

Comprehension Score Boxes

Progress Graph: Passages 26–50

Directions: Write your Total Score for each passage in the comprehension score box under the number of the passage. Then plot your score on the graph itself by putting a small *x* on the line directly above the number of the passage, across from the score you got for that passage. As you mark your score for each passage, graph your progress by drawing a line to connect the *x*'s.

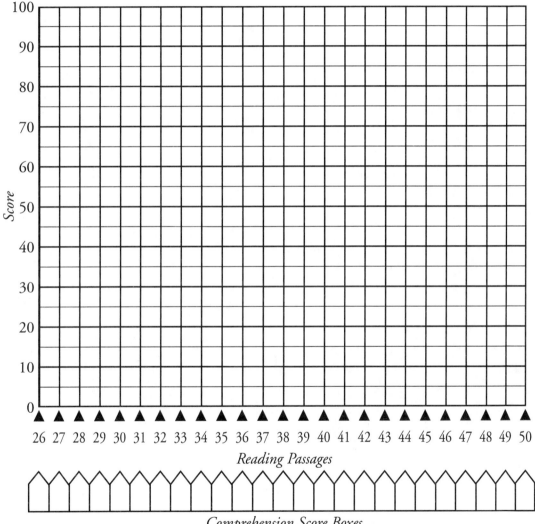

Reading Passages

Comprehension Score Boxes

Progress Graph: Passages 51–75

Directions: Write your Total Score for each passage in the comprehension score box under the number of the passage. Then plot your score on the graph itself by putting a small *x* on the line directly above the number of the passage, across from the score you got for that passage. As you mark your score for each passage, graph your progress by drawing a line to connect the *x*'s.

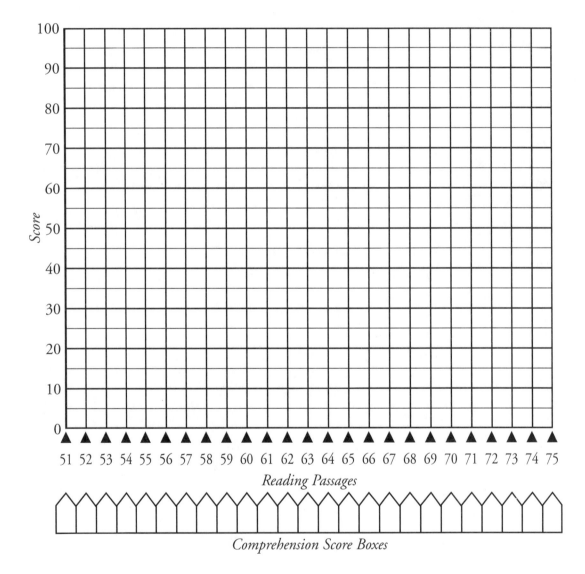

Reading Passages

Comprehension Score Boxes